MznLnx

Missing Links Exam Preps

Exam Prep for

Corporate Finance: A Practical Approach

Robinson, Fridson & Troughton, 1st Edition

The MznLnx Exam Prep is your link from the texbook and lecture to your exams.
The MznLnx Exam Preps are unauthorized and comprehensive reviews of your textbooks.

MznLnx

Rico
Publications

Exam Prep for Corporate Finance: A Practical Approach
1st Edition
Robinson, Fridson & Troughton

Publisher: Raymond Houge
Assistant Editor: Michael Rouger
Text and Cover Designer: Lisa Buckner
Marketing Manager: Sara Swagger
Project Manager, Editorial Production: Jerry Emerson
Art Director: Vernon Lowerui

Product Manager: Dave Mason
Editorial Assitant: Rachel Guzmanji
Pedagogy: Debra Long
Cover Image: Jim Reed/Getty Images
Text and Cover Printer: City Printing, Inc.
Compositor: Media Mix, Inc.

Printed in the United States
ISBN:

For more information about our products, contact us at:
Dave.Mason@RicoPublications.com

For permission to use material from this text or product, submit a request online to:
Dave.Mason@RicoPublications.com

Contents

TO THE STUDENT

COMPREHENSIVE

The *MznLnx* Exam Prep series is designed to help you pass your exams. Editors at MznLnx review your textbooks and then prepare these practice exams to help you master the textbook material. Unlike study guides, workbooks, and practice tests provided by the texbook publisher and textbook authors, *MznLnx* gives you ***all*** of the material in each chapter in exam form, not just samples, so you can be sure to nail your exam.

MECHANICAL

The MznLnx Exam Prep series creates exams that will help you learn the subject matter as well as test you on your understanding. Each question is designed to help you master the concept. Just working through the exams, you gain an understanding of the subject--its a simple mechanical process that produces success.

INTEGRATED STUDY GUIDE AND REVIEW

MznLnx is not just a set of exams designed to test you, its also a comprehensive review of the subject content. Each exam question is also a review of the concept, making sure that you will get the answer correct without having to go to other sources of material. You learn as you go! Its the easiest way to pass an exam.

HUMOR

Studying can be tedious and dry. MznLnx's instructional design includes moderate humor within the exam questions on occassion, to break the tedium and revitalize the brain

1. The institution most often referenced by the word '_________' is a public or publicly traded _________, the shares of which are traded on a public stock exchange (e.g., the New York Stock Exchange or Nasdaq in the United States) where shares of stock of _________s are bought and sold by and to the general public. Most of the largest businesses in the world are publicly traded _________s. However, the majority of _________s are said to be closely held, privately held or close _________s, meaning that no ready market exists for the trading of shares.
   a. Protect
   b. Corporation
   c. Federal Home Loan Mortgage Corporation
   d. Depository Trust Company

2. An _________ is a risk arising from execution of a company's business functions. As such, it is a very broad concept including e.g. fraud risks, legal risks, physical or environmental risks, etc. The term _________ is most commonly found in risk management programs of financial institutions that must organize their risk management program according to Basel II.
   a. Operational risk
   b. ABN Amro
   c. AAB
   d. A Random Walk Down Wall Street

3. _________ is a fee paid on borrowed assets. It is the price paid for the use of borrowed money , or, money earned by deposited funds . Assets that are sometimes lent with _________ include money, shares, consumer goods through hire purchase, major assets such as aircraft, and even entire factories in finance lease arrangements.
   a. A Random Walk Down Wall Street
   b. Insolvency
   c. AAB
   d. Interest

4. _________ is the set of processes, customs, policies, laws and institutions affecting the way a corporation is directed, administered or controlled. _________ also includes the relationships among the many stakeholders involved and the goals for which the corporation is governed. The principal stakeholders are the shareholders, management and the board of directors.
   a. Corporate governance
   b. Due diligence
   c. Foreign Corrupt Practices Act
   d. Patent

5. A _________ is a pool of assets forming an independent legal entity that are bought with the contributions to a pension plan for the exclusive purpose of financing pension plan benefits.

_________s are important shareholders of listed and private companies. They are especially important to the stock market where large institutional investors like the Ontario Teachers' Pension Plan dominate.

a. Leveraged buyout
b. Limited liability company
c. Leverage
d. Pension fund

6. A sole _________, or simply _________ is a type of business entity which legally has no separate existence from its owner. Hence, the limitations of liability enjoyed by a corporation and limited liability partnerships do not apply to sole proprietors. All debts of the business are debts of the owner.

a. Product life cycle
b. Free cash flow
c. Just-in-time
d. Proprietorship

7. A _________ is a type of business entity in which partners (owners) share with each other the profits or losses of the business undertaking in which all have invested. _________s are often favored over corporations for taxation purposes, as the _________ structure does not generally incur a tax on profits before it is distributed to the partners (i.e. there is no dividend tax levied.) However, depending on the _________ structure and the jurisdiction in which it operates, owners of a _________ may be exposed to greater personal liability than they would as shareholders of a corporation.

a. National Securities Markets Improvement Act of 1996
b. Fiduciary
c. Clayton Antitrust Act
d. Partnership

8. A mutual shareholder or _________ is an individual or company (including a corporation) that legally owns one or more shares of stock in a joint stock company. A company's shareholders collectively own that company. Thus, the typical goal of such companies is to enhance shareholder value.

a. Stock market bubble
b. Stockholder
c. Trading curb
d. Limit order

9. In the most general sense, a _________ is anything that is a hindrance, or puts individuals at a disadvantage.

Before we discuss the financial terms, we should note that a _________ can also have a much more important slang meaning.

This is best described in an example.

a. McFadden Act
b. Covenant
c. Liability
d. Limited liability

10. _________ is a concept whereby a person's financial liability is limited to a fixed sum, most commonly the value of a person's investment in a company or partnership with _________. A shareholder in a limited company is not personally liable for any of the debts of the company, other than for the value of his investment in that company. The same is true for the members of a _________ partnership and the limited partners in a limited partnership.

a. Personal property
b. Beneficial owner
c. Sarbanes-Oxley Act
d. Limited liability

11. In political science and economics, the _________ or agency dilemma treats the difficulties that arise under conditions of incomplete and asymmetric information when a principal hires an agent. Various mechanisms may be used to try to align the interests of the agent with those of the principal, such as piece rates/commissions, profit sharing, efficiency wages, performance measurement (including financial statements), the agent posting a bond, or fear of firing. The _________ is found in most employer/employee relationships, for example, when stockholders hire top executives of corporations.

a. 4-4-5 Calendar
b. Principal-agent problem
c. 7-Eleven
d. 529 plan

12. In accounting, _________ refers to the portion of net income which is retained by the corporation rather than distributed to its owners as dividends. Similarly, if the corporation makes a loss, then that loss is retained and called variously retained losses, accumulated losses or accumulated deficit. _________ and losses are cumulative from year to year with losses offsetting earnings.

a. Retained earnings
b. Generally Accepted Accounting Principles
c. Matching principle
d. Historical cost

13. An _________ is a document a company presents at an annual general meeting for approval by its shareholders, or a charitable organization presents its trustees. The report is made up of reports, which may include the following:

- Chairman's report
- CEO's report
- Auditor's report on corporate governance
- Mission statement
- Corporate governance statement of compliance
- Statement of directors' responsibilities
- Invitation to the company's AGM

as well as financial statements including:

- Auditor's report on the financial statements
- Balance sheet
- Statement of retained earnings
- Income statement
- Cash flow statement
- Notes to the financial statements
- Accounting policies

Other information deemed relevant to stakeholders may be included, such as a report on operations for manufacturing firms. In the case of larger companies, it is usually a sleek, colorful, high gloss publication.

The details provided in the report are of use to investors to understand the company's financial position and future direction.

a. Outstanding balance
b. Amortization schedule
c. Annual report
d. Accrued liabilities

14. A _________ is a statement required of a United States firm when soliciting shareholder votes. The firm needs to file a _________ with the U.S. Securities and Exchange Commission. This statement is useful in assessing how management is paid and potential conflict-of-interest issues with auditors.

a. 529 plan
b. Proxy Statement
c. 4-4-5 Calendar
d. 7-Eleven

15. The U.S. _________ is an independent agency of the United States government which holds primary responsibility for enforcing the federal securities laws and regulating the securities industry, the nation's stock and options exchanges, and other electronic securities markets. The SEC was created by section 4 of the SEC of 1934 (now codified as 15 U.S.C. Â§ 78d and commonly referred to as the 1934 Act.)
a. 7-Eleven
b. 4-4-5 Calendar
c. Securities and Exchange Commission
d. 529 plan

16. A _________ is a fungible, negotiable instrument representing financial value. They are broadly categorized into debt securities (such as banknotes, bonds and debentures), and equity securities; e.g., common stocks. The company or other entity issuing the _________ is called the issuer.
a. Securities lending
b. Tracking stock
c. Book entry
d. Security

17. An _________ is a company whose main business is holding securities of other companies purely for investment purposes. The _________ invests money on behalf of its shareholders who in turn share in the profits and losses.
a. AAB
b. A Random Walk Down Wall Street
c. Investment Company
d. Unit investment trust

18. _________ is the balance of the amounts of cash being received and paid by a business during a defined period of time, sometimes tied to a specific project. Measurement of _________ can be used

- to evaluate the state or performance of a business or project.
- to determine problems with liquidity. Being profitable does not necessarily mean being liquid. A company can fail because of a shortage of cash, even while profitable.
- to generate project rate of returns. The time of _________s into and out of projects are used as inputs to financial models such as internal rate of return, and net present value.
- to examine income or growth of a business when it is believed that accrual accounting concepts do not represent economic realities. Alternately, _________ can be used to 'validate' the net income generated by accrual accounting.

_________ as a generic term may be used differently depending on context, and certain _________ definitions may be adapted by analysts and users for their own uses. Common terms include operating _________ and free _________.

_________s can be classified into:

1. Operational _________s: Cash received or expended as a result of the company's core business activities.
2. Investment _________s: Cash received or expended through capital expenditure, investments or acquisitions.
3. Financing _________s: Cash received or expended as a result of financial activities, such as interests and dividends.

All three together - the net _________ - are necessary to reconcile the beginning cash balance to the ending cash balance. Loan draw downs or equity injections, that is just shifting of capital but no expenditure as such, are not considered in the net _________.

a. Cash flow
b. Shareholder value
c. Real option
d. Corporate finance

19. In a publicly-held company, an _________ is an operating committee of the Board of Directors, typically charged with oversight of financial reporting and disclosure. Committee members are drawn from members of the Company's board of directors, with a Chairperson selected from among the members. An _________ of a publicly-traded company in the United States is composed of independent and outside directors referred to as non-executive directors, at least one of which is typically a financial expert.

a. Attestation Standards
b. Audit working paper
c. Audit committee
d. Audit management

20. A _________ is a group formed usually from inside the membership of an organization for the purpose of nominating candidates for office within the organization. It works similarly to an electoral college, the main difference being that the available candidates, either nominated or 'written in' outside of the committee's choices, are then voted into office by all of the members. The system is a part of governance methods often employed by corporate bodies, business entities, and social and sporting groups - especially clubs.

a. Nominating committee
b. 4-4-5 Calendar
c. 529 plan
d. 7-Eleven

21. The _________ is a stock exchange based in New York City, New York. It is the largest stock exchange in the world by dollar value of its listed companies securities. As of October 2008, the combined capitalization of all domestic _________ listed companies was $10.1 trillion.

a. 7-Eleven
b. 529 plan
c. 4-4-5 Calendar
d. New York Stock Exchange

22. A _________, securities exchange or (in Europe) bourse is a corporation or mutual organization which provides 'trading' facilities for stock brokers and traders, to trade stocks and other securities. _________s also provide facilities for the issue and redemption of securities as well as other financial instruments and capital events including the payment of income and dividends. The securities traded on a _________ include: shares issued by companies, unit trusts and other pooled investment products and bonds.

a. 529 plan
b. 4-4-5 Calendar
c. 7-Eleven
d. Stock Exchange

23. An _________ is a contract written by a seller that conveys to the buyer the right -- but not the obligation -- to buy (in the case of a call _________) or to sell (in the case of a put _________) a particular asset, such as a piece of property such as, among others, a futures contract. In return for granting the _________, the seller collects a payment (the premium) from the buyer.

For example, buying a call _________ provides the right to buy a specified quantity of a security at a set strike price at some time on or before expiration, while buying a put _________ provides the right to sell.

a. Annuity
b. Amortization
c. AT'T Mobility LLC
d. Option

24. An _________ option has no intrinsic value. A call option is _________ when the strike price is above the spot price of the underlying security. A put option is _________ when the strike price is below the spot price.
a. AAB
b. ABN Amro
c. A Random Walk Down Wall Street
d. Out-of-the-money

25. _________ refers to stock of a company that is not fully transferable until certain conditions have been met. Upon satisfaction of those conditions, the stock becomes transferable by the person holding the award.

Another type of _________ is a form of compensation granted by a company. Typically, the conditions that allow the shares to be transferred are a period of time, when they vest.

a. Cash flow
b. Market for corporate control
c. Shareholder value
d. Restricted stock

26. The term _________ is a term applied to practices that are perfunctory, or seek to satisfy the minimum requirements or to conform to a convention or doctrine. It has different meanings in different fields.

In accounting, _________ earnings are those earnings of companies in addition to actual earnings calculated under the Generally Accepted Accounting Principles (GAAP) in their quarterly and yearly financial reports.

a. Long-term liabilities
b. Deferred financing costs
c. Pro forma
d. Deferred income

27. A _________, reserve bank, or monetary authority is the entity responsible for the monetary policy of a country or of a group of member states. It is a bank that can lend money to other banks in times of need. Its primary responsibility is to maintain the stability of the national currency and money supply, but more active duties include controlling subsidized-loan interest rates, and acting as a lender of last resort to the banking sector during times of financial crisis (private banks often being integral to the national financial system.)

a. 4-4-5 Calendar
b. Central bank
c. 7-Eleven
d. 529 plan

28. The _________ is a protocol to the United Nations Framework Convention on Climate Change (UNFCCC or FCCC), an international environmental treaty produced at the United Nations Conference on Environment and Development (UNCED), informally known as the Earth Summit, held in Rio de Janeiro, Brazil, from 3-14 June 1992. The treaty is intended to achieve 'stabilization of greenhouse gas concentrations in the atmosphere at a level that would prevent dangerous anthropogenic interference with the climate system.' The _________ establishes legally binding commitments for the reduction of four greenhouse gases (carbon dioxide, methane, nitrous oxide, sulfur hexafluoride), and two groups of gases (hydrofluorocarbons and perfluorocarbons) produced by 'Annex I' (industrialized) nations, as well as general commitments for all member countries. As of 2008, 183 parties have ratified the protocol, which was initially adopted for use on 11 December 1997 in Kyoto, Japan and which entered into force on 16 February 2005.

a. Personal carbon trading
b. Carbon offset
c. Joint Implementation
d. Kyoto Protocol

29. _________: Sometimes governments change the law in a way that adversely affects a bank's position.

The Risk Principle is an area of law closely tied to legal causation in negligence. It provides limits on negligence for harm caused unforeseeably.

a. Flow to Equity-Approach
b. Federal Work Study program
c. Legal and regulatory risk
d. Price channel

30. _________ is normally any risk associated with any form of financing.

Depending on the nature of the investment, the type of 'investment' risk will vary. High risk investments have greater potential rewards, but you may lose your money instead by taking the risk for more money.

a. Revaluation
b. Stock market index option
c. Liquidating dividend
d. Financial risk

31. _________ is the potential that negative publicity regarding an institution's business practices, whether true or not, will cause a decline in the customer base, costly litigation, or revenue reductions. Legal risk arises from the potential that unenforceable contracts, lawsuits, or adverse judgements can disrupt or otherwise negatively affect the operations or condition of a banking organization.
a. Flow to Equity-Approach
b. Board of Audit
c. Reputational risk
d. The Goodyear Tire ' Rubber Company

32. In finance, _________ is the process of estimating the potential market value of a financial asset or liability. they can be done on assets (for example, investments in marketable securities such as stocks, options, business enterprises, or intangible assets such as patents and trademarks) or on liabilities (e.g., Bonds issued by a company.) _________s are required in many contexts including investment analysis, capital budgeting, merger and acquisition transactions, financial reporting, taxable events to determine the proper tax liability, and in litigation.
a. Share
b. Procter ' Gamble
c. Valuation
d. Margin

33. In business and accounting, _________s are everything of value that is owned by a person or company. The balance sheet of a firm records the monetary value of the _________s owned by the firm. The two major _________ classes are tangible _________s and intangible _________s.
a. EBITDA
b. Accounts payable
c. Income
d. Asset

34. The _________ is a capital budgeting metric used by firms to decide whether they should make investments. It is an indicator of the efficiency or quality of an investment, as opposed to net present value (NPV), which indicates value or magnitude.

The IRR is the annualized effective compounded return rate which can be earned on the invested capital, i.e., the yield on the investment.

a. ABN Amro
b. AAB
c. A Random Walk Down Wall Street
d. Internal rate of return

1. _________ are made by investors and investment managers.

Investors commonly perform investment analysis by making use of fundamental analysis, technical analysis and gut feel.

_________ are often supported by decision tools.

a. Asset allocation
b. Investment decisions
c. Investing online
d. Investment performance

2. _________ is the planning process used to determine whether a firm's long term investments such as new machinery, replacement machinery, new plants, new products, and research development projects are worth pursuing. It is budget for major capital, or investment, expenditures.

Many formal methods are used in _________, including the techniques such as

- Net present value
- Profitability index
- Internal rate of return
- Modified Internal Rate of Return
- Equivalent annuity

These methods use the incremental cash flows from each potential investment, or project. Techniques based on accounting earnings and accounting rules are sometimes used - though economists consider this to be improper - such as the accounting rate of return, and 'return on investment.' Simplified and hybrid methods are used as well, such as payback period and discounted payback period.

a. Shareholder value
b. Financial distress
c. Preferred stock
d. Capital budgeting

3. _________ is the balance of the amounts of cash being received and paid by a business during a defined period of time, sometimes tied to a specific project. Measurement of _________ can be used

- to evaluate the state or performance of a business or project.
- to determine problems with liquidity. Being profitable does not necessarily mean being liquid. A company can fail because of a shortage of cash, even while profitable.
- to generate project rate of returns. The time of _________s into and out of projects are used as inputs to financial models such as internal rate of return, and net present value.
- to examine income or growth of a business when it is believed that accrual accounting concepts do not represent economic realities. Alternately, _________ can be used to 'validate' the net income generated by accrual accounting.

_________ as a generic term may be used differently depending on context, and certain _________ definitions may be adapted by analysts and users for their own uses. Common terms include operating _________ and free _________.

_________s can be classified into:

1. Operational _________s: Cash received or expended as a result of the company's core business activities.
2. Investment _________s: Cash received or expended through capital expenditure, investments or acquisitions.
3. Financing _________s: Cash received or expended as a result of financial activities, such as interests and dividends.

All three together - the net _________ - are necessary to reconcile the beginning cash balance to the ending cash balance. Loan draw downs or equity injections, that is just shifting of capital but no expenditure as such, are not considered in the net _________.

a. Shareholder value
b. Cash flow
c. Corporate finance
d. Real option

4. _________ or net present worth (NPW) is defined as the total present value (PV) of a time series of cash flows. It is a standard method for using the time value of money to appraise long-term projects. Used for capital budgeting, and widely throughout economics, it measures the excess or shortfall of cash flows, in present value terms, once financing charges are met.

a. Present value of costs
b. Negative gearing
c. Tax shield
d. Net present value

5. In economics, business, and accounting, a _________ is the value of money that has been used up to produce something, and hence is not available for use anymore. In business, the _________ may be one of acquisition, in which case the amount of money expended to acquire it is counted as _________. In this case, money is the input that is gone in order to acquire the thing.

a. Marginal cost
b. Sliding scale fees
c. Cost
d. Fixed costs

6. The _________ is an expected return that the provider of capital plans to earn on their investment.

Capital (money) used for funding a business should earn returns for the capital providers who risk their capital. For an investment to be worthwhile, the expected return on capital must be greater than the _________.

a. Cost of capital
b. Capital intensity
c. 4-4-5 Calendar
d. Weighted average cost of capital

7. _________ is the value on a given date of a future payment or series of future payments, discounted to reflect the time value of money and other factors such as investment risk. _________ calculations are widely used in business and economics to provide a means to compare cash flows at different times on a meaningful 'like to like' basis.

The most commonly applied model of the time value of money is compound interest.

a. Negative gearing
b. Present value of benefits
c. Net present value
d. Present value

8. In economics, an _________ or spillover of an economic transaction is an impact on a party that is not directly involved in the transaction. In such a case, prices do not reflect the full costs or benefits in production or consumption of a product or service. A positive impact is called an external benefit, while a negative impact is called an external cost.

a. A Random Walk Down Wall Street
b. AAB
c. ABN Amro
d. Externality

9. _________ or economic opportunity loss is the value of the next best alternative foregone as the result of making a decision. _________ analysis is an important part of a company's decision-making processes but is not treated as an actual cost in any financial statement. The next best thing that a person can engage in is referred to as the _________ of doing the best thing and ignoring the next best thing to be done.

a. ABN Amro
b. Opportunity cost
c. AAB
d. A Random Walk Down Wall Street

10. In economics and business decision-making, _________ are costs that cannot be recovered once they have been incurred. _________ are sometimes contrasted with variable costs, which are the costs that will change due to the proposed course of action, and prospective costs which are costs that will be incurred if an action is taken. In microeconomic theory, only variable costs are relevant to a decision.

a. Hyperbolic discounting
b. Hindsight bias
c. 4-4-5 Calendar
d. Sunk costs

11. In marketing and strategy, _________ refers to a reduction in the sales volume, sales revenue, or market share of one product as a result of the introduction of a new product by the same producer.

For example, if Coca Cola were to introduce a similar product (say, Diet Coke or Cherry Coke), this new product could take some of the sales away from the original Coke. _________ is a key consideration in product portfolio analysis.

a. 4-4-5 Calendar
b. 529 plan
c. 7-Eleven
d. Cannibalization

12. In finance, _________, also known as return on investment is the ratio of money gained or lost on an investment relative to the amount of money invested. The amount of money gained or lost may be referred to as interest, profit/loss, gain/loss, or net income/loss. The money invested may be referred to as the asset, capital, principal, or the cost basis of the investment.

a. Stock or scrip dividends
b. Composiition of Creditors
c. Doctrine of the Proper Law
d. Rate of return

13. The _________ is a capital budgeting metric used by firms to decide whether they should make investments. It is an indicator of the efficiency or quality of an investment, as opposed to net present value (NPV), which indicates value or magnitude.

The IRR is the annualized effective compounded return rate which can be earned on the invested capital, i.e., the yield on the investment.

a. A Random Walk Down Wall Street
b. Internal rate of return
c. ABN Amro
d. AAB

14. _________ in business and economics refers to the period of time required for the return on an investment to 'repay' the sum of the original investment. For example, a $1000 investment which returned $500 per year would have a two year _________. It intuitively measures how long something takes to 'pay for itself.' _________ is widely used due to its ease of use despite recognized limitations.

a. Payback period
b. Seasoned equity offering
c. Financial Gerontology
d. Consignment stock

15. _________ identifies the relationship of investment to payoff of a proposed project. The ratio is calculated as follows:

- >

_________ is also known as Profit Investment Ratio, abbreviated to P.I. and Value Investment Ratio (V.I.R.). _________ is a good tool for ranking projects because it allows you to clearly identify the amount of value created per unit of investment, thus if you are capital constrained you wish to invest in those projects which create value most efficiently first.

a. Profitability index
b. Capitalization rate
c. Conditional prepayment rate
d. Total return

16. A _________ is the price of a single share of a no. of saleable stocks of the company. Once the stock is purchased, the owner becomes a shareholder of the company that issued the share.

a. Whisper numbers
b. Trading curb
c. Stock split
d. Share price

17. _________ refers to any one of several methods by which a company, for 'financial accounting' and/or tax purposes, depreciates a fixed asset in such a way that the amount of depreciation taken each year is higher during the earlier years of an asset's life. For financial accounting purposes, _________ is generally used when an asset is expected to be much more productive during its early years, so that depreciation expense will more accurately represent how much of an asset's usefulness is being used up each year. For tax purposes, _________ provides a way of deferring corporate income taxes by reducing taxable income in current years, in exchange for increased taxable income in future years.
a. A Random Walk Down Wall Street
b. AAB
c. ABN Amro
d. Accelerated depreciation

18. _________ is a term used in accounting, economics and finance to spread the cost of an asset over the span of several years.

In simple words we can say that _________ is the reduction in the value of an asset due to usage, passage of time, wear and tear, technological outdating or obsolescence, depletion or other such factors.

In accounting, _________ is a term used to describe any method of attributing the historical or purchase cost of an asset across its useful life, roughly corresponding to normal wear and tear.

a. Bottom line
b. Depreciation
c. Deferred financing costs
d. Matching principle

19. The _________ is the current method of accelerated asset depreciation required by the United States income tax code. Under _________, all assets are divided into classes which dictate the number of years over which an asset's cost will be recovered.

Prior to the Accelerated Cost Recovery System (ACRS), most capital purchases were depreciated using a straight line technique, that allowed for the depreciation of the asset over its useful life.

a. Modified Accelerated Cost Recovery System
b. 7-Eleven
c. 4-4-5 Calendar
d. 529 plan

20. Depreciation methods that provide for a higher depreciation charge in the first year of an asset's life and gradually decreasing charges in subsequent years are called accelerated depreciation methods. This may be a more realistic reflection of an asset's actual expected benefit from the use of the asset: many assets are most useful when they are new. One popular accelerated method is the declining-balance method. Under this method the Book Value is multiplied by a fixed rate.

The most common rate used is double the straight-line rate. For this reason, this technique is referred to as the _________. To illustrate, suppose a business has an asset with $1,000 Original Cost, $100 Salvage Value, and 5 years useful life. First, calculate straight-line depreciation rate. Since the asset has 5 years useful life, the straight-line depreciation rate equals (100% / 5) 20% per year. With _________, as the name suggests, double that rate, or 40% depreciation rate is used.

a. Database auditing
b. Doctrine of the Proper Law
c. The Goodyear Tire ' Rubber Company
d. Double-declining-balance method

21. In economics, _________ is a rise in the general level of prices of goods and services in an economy over a period of time. The term '_________' once referred to increases in the money supply (monetary _________); however, economic debates about the relationship between money supply and price levels have led to its primary use today in describing price _________. _________ can also be described as a decline in the real value of money--a loss of purchasing power in the medium of exchange which is also the monetary unit of account.

a. A Random Walk Down Wall Street
b. ABN Amro
c. AAB
d. Inflation

22. An _________ can be defined as a contract which provides an income stream in return for an initial payment.

An immediate _________ is an _________ for which the time between the contract date and the date of the first payment is not longer than the time interval between payments. A common use for an immediate _________ is to provide a pension to a retired person or persons.

a. AT'T Inc.
b. Annuity
c. Intrinsic value
d. Amortization

23. A '_________' is a 'Charge' that is paid to obtain the right to delay a payment. Essentially, the payer purchases the right to make a given payment in the future instead of in the Present. The '_________', or 'Charge' that must be paid to delay the payment, is simply the difference between what the payment amount would be if it were paid in the present and what the payment amount would be paid if it were paid in the future.
a. Risk modeling
b. Value at risk
c. Discount
d. Risk aversion

24. The _________ is an interest rate a central bank charges depository institutions that borrow reserves from it.

The term _________ has two meanings:

- the same as interest rate; the term 'discount' does not refer to the meaning of the word, but to the purpose of using the quantity, such as computations of present value, e.g. net present value / discounted cash flow

- the annual effective _________, which is the annual interest divided by the capital including that interest; this rate is lower than the interest rate; it corresponds to using the value after a year as the nominal value, and seeing the initial value as the nominal value minus a discount; it is used for Treasury Bills and similar financial instruments

The annual effective _________ is the annual interest divided by the capital including that interest, which is the interest rate divided by 100% plus the interest rate. It is the annual discount factor to be applied to the future cash flow, to find the discount, subtracted from a future value to find the value one year earlier.

For example, suppose there is a government bond that sells for $95 and pays $100 in a year's time.

a. Black-Scholes
b. Fisher equation
c. Discount rate
d. Stochastic volatility

25. _________ is the risk that the value of an investment will decrease due to moves in market factors. The five standard _________ factors are:

- Equity risk, the risk that stock prices will change.
- Interest rate risk, the risk that interest rates will change.
- Currency risk, the risk that foreign exchange rates will change.
- Commodity risk, the risk that commodity prices (e.g. grains, metals) will change.

As with other forms of risk, _________ may be measured in a number of ways. Traditionally, this is done using a Value at Risk methodology. Value at risk is well established as a risk management technique, but it contains a number of limiting assumptions that constrain its accuracy.

a. Currency risk
b. Tracking error
c. Transaction risk
d. Market risk

26. _________ is the study of how the variation (uncertainty) in the output of a mathematical model can be apportioned, qualitatively or quantitatively, to different sources of variation in the input of a model .

In more general terms uncertainty and sensitivity analyses investigate the robustness of a study when the study includes some form of mathematical modelling. While uncertainty analysis studies the overall uncertainty in the conclusions of the study, _________ tries to identify what source of uncertainty weights more on the study's conclusions.

a. Proxy fight
b. Golden parachute
c. Sensitivity analysis
d. Synthetic CDO

27. _________ is a process of analyzing possible future events by considering alternative possible outcomes (scenarios.) The analysis is designed to allow improved decision-making by allowing consideration of outcomes and their implications.

For example, in economics and finance, a financial institution might attempt to forecast several possible scenarios for the economy (e.g. rapid growth, moderate growth, slow growth) and it might also attempt to forecast financial market returns (for bonds, stocks and cash) in each of those scenarios.

a. Scenario analysis
b. 4-4-5 Calendar
c. Detection Risk
d. 529 plan

28. The institution most often referenced by the word '_________' is a public or publicly traded _________, the shares of which are traded on a public stock exchange (e.g., the New York Stock Exchange or Nasdaq in the United States) where shares of stock of _________s are bought and sold by and to the general public. Most of the largest businesses in the world are publicly traded _________s. However, the majority of _________s are said to be closely held, privately held or close _________s, meaning that no ready market exists for the trading of shares.
a. Federal Home Loan Mortgage Corporation
b. Depository Trust Company
c. Protect
d. Corporation

29. In economics and finance, _________ is the practice of taking advantage of a price differential between two or more markets: striking a combination of matching deals that capitalize upon the imbalance, the profit being the difference between the market prices. When used by academics, an _________ is a transaction that involves no negative cash flow at any probabilistic or temporal state and a positive cash flow in at least one state; in simple terms, a risk-free profit.
a. Issuer
b. Initial margin
c. Arbitrage
d. Efficient-market hypothesis

30. _________ , in finance, is a general theory of asset pricing, that has become influential in the pricing of stocks.

_________ holds that the expected return of a financial asset can be modeled as a linear function of various macro-economic factors or theoretical market indices, where sensitivity to changes in each factor is represented by a factor-specific beta coefficient. The model-derived rate of return will then be used to price the asset correctly - the asset price should equal the expected end of period price discounted at the rate implied by model.

a. Arbitrage pricing theory
b. ABN Amro
c. A Random Walk Down Wall Street
d. AAB

31. The term _________ has three unrelated technical definitions, and is also used in a variety of non-technical ways.

- In financial economics, it refers to any asset used to make money, as opposed to assets used for personal enjoyment or consumption. This is an important distinction because two people can disagree sharply about the value of personal assets, one person might think a sports car is more valuable than a pickup truck, another person might have the opposite taste. But if an asset is held for the purpose of making money, taste has nothing to do with it, only differences of opinion about how much money the asset will produce. With the further assumption that people agree on the probability distribution of future cash flows, it is possible to have an objective _________ pricing model. Even without the assumption of agreement, it is possible to set rational limits on _________ value.
- In governmental accounting, it is defined as any asset used in operations with an initial useful life extending beyond one reporting period. Generally, government managers have a 'stewardship' duty to maintain _________s under their control. See International Public Sector Accounting Standards for details.
- In US tax accounting, it is defined as any property other than a list of exceptions. The main exceptions are anything held for sale, and any real estate or depreciable property used in business. Almost everything you own and use for personal purposes, pleasure or investment is a _________. If something is a _________ for tax purposes, gains or losses on sale or disposition are capital gains or capital losses. For individuals, however, capital losses on property held for personal use are generally not deductible. See the IRS publication Tax Facts about Capital Gains and Losses for details.

A well-known financial accounting textbook advises that the term be avoided except in tax accounting because it is used in so many different senses, not all of them well-defined. For example it is often used as a synonym for fixed assets or for investments in securities.

A common non-technical usage occurs when people ask that employees or the environment or something else be treated as a _________.

a. Settlement date
b. Solvency
c. Political risk
d. Capital asset

32. In finance, the _________ is used to determine a theoretically appropriate required rate of return of an asset, if that asset is to be added to an already well-diversified portfolio, given that asset's non-diversifiable risk. The model takes into account the asset's sensitivity to non-diversifiable risk (also known as systemic risk or market risk), often represented by the quantity beta (β) in the financial industry, as well as the expected return of the market and the expected return of a theoretical risk-free asset.

The model was introduced by Jack Treynor (1961, 1962), William Sharpe (1964), John Lintner (1965a,b) and Jan Mossin (1966) independently, building on the earlier work of Harry Markowitz on diversification and modern portfolio theory.

a. Cox-Ingersoll-Ross model
b. Capital asset pricing model
c. Hull-White model
d. Random walk hypothesis

33. A _________ is a fungible, negotiable instrument representing financial value. They are broadly categorized into debt securities (such as banknotes, bonds and debentures), and equity securities; e.g., common stocks. The company or other entity issuing the _________ is called the issuer.
a. Tracking stock
b. Book entry
c. Securities lending
d. Security

34. In Modern Portfolio Theory, the _________ is the graphical representation of the Capital Asset Pricing Model. It displays the expected rate of return for an overall market as a function of systematic (non-diversifiable) risk (beta.)

The Y-Intercept (beta=0) of the _________ is equal to the risk-free interest rate.

a. Certificate in Investment Performance Measurement
b. Divestment
c. Rebalancing
d. Security market line

35. In business and accounting, _________s are everything of value that is owned by a person or company. The balance sheet of a firm records the monetary value of the _________s owned by the firm. The two major _________ classes are tangible _________s and intangible _________s.
a. Accounts payable
b. EBITDA
c. Income
d. Asset

36. In finance, _________ is the process of estimating the potential market value of a financial asset or liability. they can be done on assets (for example, investments in marketable securities such as stocks, options, business enterprises, or intangible assets such as patents and trademarks) or on liabilities (e.g., Bonds issued by a company.) _________s are required in many contexts including investment analysis, capital budgeting, merger and acquisition transactions, financial reporting, taxable events to determine the proper tax liability, and in litigation.

a. Margin
b. Procter ' Gamble
c. Share
d. Valuation

37. The _________ is the rate that a company is expected to pay to finance its assets. WACC is the minimum return that a company must earn on existing asset base to satisfy its creditors, owners, and other providers of capital.

Companies raise money from a number of sources: common equity, preferred equity, straight debt, convertible debt, exchangeable debt, warrants, options, pension liabilities, executive stock options, governmental subsidies, and so on.

a. Capital intensity
b. Cost of capital
c. 4-4-5 Calendar
d. Weighted average cost of capital

38. In corporate finance, _________ analysis applies put option and call option valuation techniques to capital budgeting decisions. A _________ itself, is the right--but not the obligation--to undertake some business decision; typically the option to make, or abandon, a capital investment. For example, the opportunity to invest in the expansion of a firm's factory, or alternatively to sell the factory, is a _________.

a. Real option
b. Cash flow
c. Book building
d. Capital budgeting

39. An _________ is a contract written by a seller that conveys to the buyer the right -- but not the obligation -- to buy (in the case of a call _________) or to sell (in the case of a put _________) a particular asset, such as a piece of property such as, among others, a futures contract. In return for granting the _________, the seller collects a payment (the premium) from the buyer.

For example, buying a call _________ provides the right to buy a specified quantity of a security at a set strike price at some time on or before expiration, while buying a put _________ provides the right to sell.

a. AT'T Mobility LLC
b. Option
c. Amortization
d. Annuity

40. A _________ is a decision support tool that uses a tree-like graph or model of decisions and their possible consequences, including chance event outcomes, resource costs, and utility. _________s are commonly used in operations research, specifically in decision analysis, to help identify a strategy most likely to reach a goal. Another use of _________s is as a descriptive means for calculating conditional probabilities.

a. 7-Eleven
b. 4-4-5 Calendar
c. 529 plan
d. Decision tree

41. In finance, the _________ approach describes a method of valuing a project, company, or asset using the concepts of the time value of money. All future cash flows are estimated and discounted to give their present values. The discount rate used is generally the appropriate cost of capital and may incorporate judgments of the uncertainty (riskiness) of the future cash flows.

a. Future-oriented
b. Discounted cash flow
c. Net present value
d. Present value of benefits

42. _________ are the earnings returned on the initial investment amount.

In the US, the Financial Accounting Standards Board (FASB) requires companies' income statements to report _________ for each of the major categories of the income statement: continuing operations, discontinued operations, extraordinary items, and net income.

The _________ formula does not include preferred dividends for categories outside of continued operations and net income.

a. Inventory turnover
b. Average accounting return
c. Earnings per share
d. Assets turnover

43. _________ is equal to the income that a firm has after subtracting costs and expenses from the total revenue. _________ can be distributed among holders of common stock as a dividend or held by the firm as retained earnings. _________ is an accounting term; in some countries (such as the UK) profit is the usual term.

a. Historical cost
b. Write-off
c. Furniture, Fixtures and Equipment
d. Net income

44. _________ measures the rate of return on the ownership interest (shareholders' equity) of the common stock owners. _________ is viewed as one of the most important financial ratios. It measures a firm's efficiency at generating profits from every dollar of shareholders' equity (also known as net assets or assets minus liabilities.)
a. Return of capital
b. Diluted Earnings Per Share
c. Return on sales
d. Return on equity

45. An _________ is an economic concept that relates to the cost incurred by an entity (such as organizations) associated with problems such as divergent management-shareholder objectives and information asymmetry. The costs consist of two main sources:

1. The costs inherently associated with using an agent (e.g., the risk that agents will use organizational resource for their own benefit) and
2. The costs of techniques used to mitigate the problems associated with using an agent (e.g., the costs of producing financial statements or the use of stock options to align executive interests to shareholder interests.)

Though effects of _________ are present in any agency relationship, the term is most used in business contexts.

The information asymmetry that exists between shareholders and the Chief Executive Officer is generally considered to be a classic example of a principal-agent problem. The agent (the manager) is working on behalf of the principal (the shareholders), who does not observe the actions of the agent.

a. Agency cost
b. A Random Walk Down Wall Street
c. ABN Amro
d. AAB

46. _________, refers to consumption opportunity gained by an entity within a specified time frame, which is generally expressed in monetary terms. However, for households and individuals, '_________ is the sum of all the wages, salaries, profits, interests payments, rents and other forms of earnings received... in a given period of time.' For firms, _________ generally refers to net-profit: what remains of revenue after expenses have been subtracted.

a. Annual report
b. Accrual
c. Income
d. OIBDA

47. In business and finance, a _________ (also referred to as equity _________) of stock means a _________ of ownership in a corporation (company.) In the plural, stocks is often used as a synonym for _________s especially in the United States, but it is less commonly used that way outside of North America.

In the United Kingdom, South Africa, and Australia, stock can also refer to completely different financial instruments such as government bonds or, less commonly, to all kinds of marketable securities.

a. Share
b. Bucket shop
c. Procter ' Gamble
d. Margin

48. Pure _________ is the increase in wealth that an investor has from making an investment, taking into consideration all costs associated with that investment including the opportunity cost of capital.

A key difficulty in measuring profit is in defining costs. Pure economic monetary profits can be zero or negative even in competitive equilibrium when accounted monetized costs exceed monetized price.

a. AAB
b. Operating profit
c. A Random Walk Down Wall Street
d. Economic profit

49. _________ is the difference between price and the costs of bringing to market whatever it is that is accounted as an enterprise (whether by harvest, extraction, manufacture, or purchase) in terms of the component costs of delivered goods and/or services and any operating or other expenses.

A key difficulty in measuring profit is in defining costs. Pure economic monetary profits can be zero or negative even in competitive equilibrium when accounted monetized costs exceed monetized price.

a. AAB
b. A Random Walk Down Wall Street
c. Economic profit
d. Accounting profit

50. _________ is a rent received on a regular basis, with little effort required to maintain it. It is advocated by some authors, especially by Robert Kiyosaki.

Some examples of _________ are:

- Repeated regular income, earned by a sales person, generated from the payment of a product or service that must be renewed on a regular basis, in order to continue receiving its benefits - also called residual income.
- Rental from property;
- Royalties from publishing a book or from licensing a patent or other form of intellectual property;
- Earnings from internet advertisement on your websites;
- Earnings from a business that does not require direct involvement from the owner or merchant;
- Dividend and interest income from owning securities, such as stocks and bonds, are usually referred to as portfolio income, which can be considered a form of _________;
- Pensions.

_________ is usually taxable. The American Internal Revenue Service defines _________ as 'any activity...

a. Fixed exchange rate system
b. 4-4-5 Calendar
c. Passive income
d. Horizontal merger

1. In economics, business, and accounting, a _________ is the value of money that has been used up to produce something, and hence is not available for use anymore. In business, the _________ may be one of acquisition, in which case the amount of money expended to acquire it is counted as _________. In this case, money is the input that is gone in order to acquire the thing.
   a. Sliding scale fees
   b. Fixed costs
   c. Marginal cost
   d. Cost

2. The _________ is an expected return that the provider of capital plans to earn on their investment.

Capital (money) used for funding a business should earn returns for the capital providers who risk their capital. For an investment to be worthwhile, the expected return on capital must be greater than the _________.

   a. Weighted average cost of capital
   b. Capital intensity
   c. 4-4-5 Calendar
   d. Cost of capital

3. In finance, _________ refers to the way a corporation finances its assets through some combination of equity, debt, or hybrid securities. A firm's _________ is then the composition or 'structure' of its liabilities. For example, a firm that sells $20 billion in equity and $80 billion in debt is said to be 20% equity-financed and 80% debt-financed.
   a. Rights issue
   b. Book building
   c. Market for corporate control
   d. Capital structure

4. _________ refers to the likelihood that changes in the business environment adversely affect operating profits or the value of assets in a specific country. For example, financial factors such as currency controls, devaluation or regulatory changes, or stability factors such as mass riots, civil war and other potential events contribute to companies' operational risks. This term is also sometimes referred to as political risk, however _________ is a more general term, which generally only refers to risks affecting all companies operating within a particular country.
   a. Solvency
   b. Capital asset
   c. Country risk
   d. Single-index model

5. In economics and finance, _________ is the change in total cost that arises when the quantity produced changes by one unit. It is the cost of producing one more unit of a good. Mathematically, the _________ function is expressed as the first derivative of the total cost (TC) function with respect to quantity (Q). Note that the _________ may change with volume, and so at each level of production, the _________ is the cost of the next unit produced.

A typical _________ Curve

>

a. Fixed costs
b. Cost accounting
c. Sliding scale fees
d. Marginal cost

6. The _________ is the rate that a company is expected to pay to finance its assets. WACC is the minimum return that a company must earn on existing asset base to satisfy its creditors, owners, and other providers of capital.

Companies raise money from a number of sources: common equity, preferred equity, straight debt, convertible debt, exchangeable debt, warrants, options, pension liabilities, executive stock options, governmental subsidies, and so on.

a. Cost of capital
b. Weighted average cost of capital
c. 4-4-5 Calendar
d. Capital intensity

7. _________ are costs incurred on the purchase of land, buildings, construction and equipment to be used in the production of goods or the rendering of services. In other words, the total cost needed to bring a project to a commercially operable status. However, _________ are not limited to the initial construction of a factory or other business.

a. Trade-off
b. Capital outflow
c. Capital costs
d. Defined contribution plan

8. _________ is the planning process used to determine whether a firm's long term investments such as new machinery, replacement machinery, new plants, new products, and research development projects are worth pursuing. It is budget for major capital, or investment, expenditures.

Many formal methods are used in _________, including the techniques such as

- Net present value
- Profitability index
- Internal rate of return
- Modified Internal Rate of Return
- Equivalent annuity

These methods use the incremental cash flows from each potential investment, or project. Techniques based on accounting earnings and accounting rules are sometimes used - though economists consider this to be improper - such as the accounting rate of return, and 'return on investment.' Simplified and hybrid methods are used as well, such as payback period and discounted payback period.

a. Financial distress
b. Preferred stock
c. Shareholder value
d. Capital budgeting

9. A _________ is a fungible, negotiable instrument representing financial value. They are broadly categorized into debt securities (such as banknotes, bonds and debentures), and equity securities; e.g., common stocks. The company or other entity issuing the _________ is called the issuer.
a. Tracking stock
b. Securities lending
c. Book entry
d. Security

10. In finance, _________ is the process of estimating the potential market value of a financial asset or liability. they can be done on assets (for example, investments in marketable securities such as stocks, options, business enterprises, or intangible assets such as patents and trademarks) or on liabilities (e.g., Bonds issued by a company.) _________s are required in many contexts including investment analysis, capital budgeting, merger and acquisition transactions, financial reporting, taxable events to determine the proper tax liability, and in litigation.
a. Margin
b. Share
c. Valuation
d. Procter ' Gamble

11. _________ or net present worth (NPW) is defined as the total present value (PV) of a time series of cash flows. It is a standard method for using the time value of money to appraise long-term projects. Used for capital budgeting, and widely throughout economics, it measures the excess or shortfall of cash flows, in present value terms, once financing charges are met.

a. Tax shield
b. Present value of costs
c. Negative gearing
d. Net present value

12. _________ is the value on a given date of a future payment or series of future payments, discounted to reflect the time value of money and other factors such as investment risk. _________ calculations are widely used in business and economics to provide a means to compare cash flows at different times on a meaningful 'like to like' basis.

The most commonly applied model of the time value of money is compound interest.

a. Present value
b. Net present value
c. Present value of benefits
d. Negative gearing

13. _________ is that which is owed; usually referencing assets owed, but the term can cover other obligations. In the case of assets, _________ is a means of using future purchasing power in the present before a summation has been earned. Some companies and corporations use _________ as a part of their overall corporate finance strategy.

a. Cross-collateralization
b. Credit cycle
c. Partial Payment
d. Debt

14. The _________ or redemption yield is the yield promised to the bondholder on the assumption that the bond or other fixed-interest security such as gilts will be held to maturity, that all coupon and principal payments will be made and coupon payments are reinvested at the bond's promised yield at the same rate as invested. It is a measure of the return of the bond. This technique in theory allows investors to calculate the fair value of different financial instruments.

a. Yield
b. Macaulay duration
c. 4-4-5 Calendar
d. Yield to maturity

15. Leasing is a process by which a firm can obtain the use of a certain fixed assets for which it must pay a series of contractual, periodic, tax deductable payments. The lessee is the receiver of the services or the assets under the lease contract and the lessor is the owner of the assets. The relationship between the tenant and the landlord is called a _________, and can be for a fixed or an indefinite period of time (called the term of the lease.)

a. Real estate investing
b. Real Estate Investment Trust
c. REIT
d. Tenancy

16. _________ is typically a higher ranking stock than voting shares, and its terms are negotiated between the corporation and the investor.

_________ usually carry no voting rights, but may carry superior priority over common stock in the payment of dividends and upon liquidation. _________ may carry a dividend that is paid out prior to any dividends to common stock holders.

a. Follow-on offering
b. Preferred stock
c. Trade-off theory
d. Second lien loan

17. An _________ is an economic concept that relates to the cost incurred by an entity (such as organizations) associated with problems such as divergent management-shareholder objectives and information asymmetry. The costs consist of two main sources:

1. The costs inherently associated with using an agent (e.g., the risk that agents will use organizational resource for their own benefit) and
2. The costs of techniques used to mitigate the problems associated with using an agent (e.g., the costs of producing financial statements or the use of stock options to align executive interests to shareholder interests.)

Though effects of _________ are present in any agency relationship, the term is most used in business contexts.

The information asymmetry that exists between shareholders and the Chief Executive Officer is generally considered to be a classic example of a principal-agent problem. The agent (the manager) is working on behalf of the principal (the shareholders), who does not observe the actions of the agent.

a. A Random Walk Down Wall Street
b. ABN Amro
c. Agency cost
d. AAB

18. In finance, a _________ is a debt security, in which the authorized issuer owes the holders a debt and, depending on the terms of the _________, is obliged to pay interest (the coupon) and/or to repay the principal at a later date, termed maturity.

Thus a _________ is a loan: the issuer is the borrower, the _________ holder is the lender, and the coupon is the interest. _________s provide the borrower with external funds to finance long-term investments, or, in the case of government _________s, to finance current expenditure.

a. Convertible bond
b. Catastrophe bonds
c. Puttable bond
d. Bond

19.

In finance, the _________ can be the expected rate of return above the risk-free interest rate. When measuring risk, a common sense approach is to compare the risk-free return on T-bills and the very risky return on other investments. The difference between these two returns can be interpreted as a measure of the excess return on the average risky asset. This excess return is known as the _________.

a. Risk aversion
b. Risk premium
c. Risk adjusted return on capital
d. Risk modeling

20. In finance, the term _________ describes the amount in cash that returns to the owners of a security. Normally it does not include the price variations, at the difference of the total return. _________ applies to various stated rates of return on stocks (common and preferred, and convertible), fixed income instruments (bonds, notes, bills, strips, zero coupon), and some other investment type insurance products (e.g. annuities.)

a. Yield
b. 4-4-5 Calendar
c. Yield to maturity
d. Macaulay duration

21. The term _________ has three unrelated technical definitions, and is also used in a variety of non-technical ways.

- In financial economics, it refers to any asset used to make money, as opposed to assets used for personal enjoyment or consumption. This is an important distinction because two people can disagree sharply about the value of personal assets, one person might think a sports car is more valuable than a pickup truck, another person might have the opposite taste. But if an asset is held for the purpose of making money, taste has nothing to do with it, only differences of opinion about how much money the asset will produce. With the further assumption that people agree on the probability distribution of future cash flows, it is possible to have an objective _________ pricing model. Even without the assumption of agreement, it is possible to set rational limits on _________ value.
- In governmental accounting, it is defined as any asset used in operations with an initial useful life extending beyond one reporting period. Generally, government managers have a 'stewardship' duty to maintain _________s under their control. See International Public Sector Accounting Standards for details.
- In US tax accounting, it is defined as any property other than a list of exceptions. The main exceptions are anything held for sale, and any real estate or depreciable property used in business. Almost everything you own and use for personal purposes, pleasure or investment is a _________. If something is a _________ for tax purposes, gains or losses on sale or disposition are capital gains or capital losses. For individuals, however, capital losses on property held for personal use are generally not deductible. See the IRS publication Tax Facts about Capital Gains and Losses for details.

A well-known financial accounting textbook advises that the term be avoided except in tax accounting because it is used in so many different senses, not all of them well-defined. For example it is often used as a synonym for fixed assets or for investments in securities.

A common non-technical usage occurs when people ask that employees or the environment or something else be treated as a _________.

a. Capital asset
b. Solvency
c. Political risk
d. Settlement date

22. In finance, the _________ is used to determine a theoretically appropriate required rate of return of an asset, if that asset is to be added to an already well-diversified portfolio, given that asset's non-diversifiable risk. The model takes into account the asset's sensitivity to non-diversifiable risk (also known as systemic risk or market risk), often represented by the quantity beta (β) in the financial industry, as well as the expected return of the market and the expected return of a theoretical risk-free asset.

The model was introduced by Jack Treynor (1961, 1962), William Sharpe (1964), John Lintner (1965a,b) and Jan Mossin (1966) independently, building on the earlier work of Harry Markowitz on diversification and modern portfolio theory.

a. Cox-Ingersoll-Ross model
b. Capital asset pricing model
c. Hull-White model
d. Random walk hypothesis

23. _________ is a term coined in 1985 by economists Rajnish Mehra and Edward C. Prescott. It is based on the observation that in order to reconcile the much higher return on equity stock compared to government bonds in the United States, individuals must have implausibly high risk aversion according to standard economics models. Similar situations prevail in many other industrialized countries.

a. Loss aversion
b. Quantitative behavioral finance
c. Perth Leadership Outcome Model
d. The equity premium puzzle

24. In business and accounting, _________s are everything of value that is owned by a person or company. The balance sheet of a firm records the monetary value of the _________s owned by the firm. The two major _________ classes are tangible _________s and intangible _________s.

a. Asset
b. Accounts payable
c. Income
d. EBITDA

25. _________ is a variant of the Discounted cash flow model, a method for valuing a stock or business. Often used to provide difficult-to-resolve valuation issues for litigation, tax planning, and business transactions that are currently off market.

It assumes that the company issues a dividend that has a current value of D that grows at a constant rate g. It also assumes that the required rate of return for the stock remains constant at k which is equal to the cost of equity for that company. It involves summing the infinite series which gives the value of price current P.

a. Stock or scrip dividends
b. Securitization
c. Gordon growth model
d. Special journals

26. The phrase _________ refers to the aspect of corporate strategy, corporate finance and management dealing with the buying, selling and combining of different companies that can aid, finance, or help a growing company in a given industry grow rapidly without having to create another business entity.

An acquisition, also known as a takeover, is the buying of one company (the 'target') by another. An acquisition may be friendly or hostile.

a. 529 plan
b. 7-Eleven
c. 4-4-5 Calendar
d. Mergers and acquisitions

27. A '_________' is a 'Charge' that is paid to obtain the right to delay a payment. Essentially, the payer purchases the right to make a given payment in the future instead of in the Present. The '_________', or 'Charge' that must be paid to delay the payment, is simply the difference between what the payment amount would be if it were paid in the present and what the payment amount would be paid if it were paid in the future.
a. Risk aversion
b. Discount
c. Risk modeling
d. Value at risk

28. A _________ is a payment made by a corporation to its shareholder members. When a corporation earns a profit or surplus, that money can be put to two uses: it can either be re-invested in the business (called retained earnings), or it can be paid to the shareholders as a _________. Many corporations retain a portion of their earnings and pay the remainder as a _________.

a. Dividend yield
b. Dividend puzzle
c. Special dividend
d. Dividend

29. In finance, _________, also known as return on investment is the ratio of money gained or lost on an investment relative to the amount of money invested. The amount of money gained or lost may be referred to as interest, profit/loss, gain/loss, or net income/loss. The money invested may be referred to as the asset, capital, principal, or the cost basis of the investment.
a. Composiition of Creditors
b. Rate of return
c. Stock or scrip dividends
d. Doctrine of the Proper Law

30. _________ is the maximum rate at which a company can grow revenue without having to invest new equity capital. If a company earns a 15% return on equity (ROE), it can grow 15% simply by reinvesting all the earnings in new opportunities and maintaining a stable debt to equity ratio. In order to grow faster, the company would have to invest more equity capital or increase its financial leverage.

a. Price/cash flow ratio
b. Current ratio
c. Return on capital employed
d. Sustainable growth rate

31. _________s is a real estate appraisal term referring to properties with characteristics that are similar to a subject property whose value is being sought. This can be accomplished either by a real estate agent who attempts to establish the value of a potential client's home or property through market analysis or, by a licensed or certified appraiser or surveyor using more defined methods, when performing a real estate appraisal.

Five factors are usually considered when determining _________s:

- Conditions of Sale -- Did the _________ recently transact under conditions (e.g. -- arms length, distress sale, estate settlement) which are consistent with the standard of value under which the appraisal is being performed?
- Financing Conditions -- Was the _________ transaction influenced by non-market or other favorable (or even unfavorable) financing terms? For example, if the _________ sold with a below-market interest rate provided by the seller, and if the standard of value (e.g. -- market value) assumes no such abnormal financing, then the appraiser may need to adjust the _________ price by an amount equal to the estimated impact of the favorable financing.
- Market Conditions -- This is often referred to as the time adjustment and accounts for changing prices over time.
- Locational Comparability -- Are the _________ and the subject property influenced by the same locational characteristics? For example, even two houses in the same neighborhood may have different views which cause one to be more valuable than the other.
- Physical Comparability -- This includes such factors as size, condition, quality, and age.

A real estate appraisal is like any other statistical sampling process. The _________s are the samples drawn and measured, and the outcome is an estimate of value -- called an 'opinion of value' in the terminology of real estate appraisal.

a. Bucket shop
b. Procter ' Gamble
c. Margin
d. Comparable

32. _________ is normally any risk associated with any form of financing.

Depending on the nature of the investment, the type of 'investment' risk will vary. High risk investments have greater potential rewards, but you may lose your money instead by taking the risk for more money.

a. Stock market index option
b. Liquidating dividend
c. Financial risk
d. Revaluation

33. _________ is the risk that the value of an investment will decrease due to moves in market factors. The five standard _________ factors are:

- Equity risk, the risk that stock prices will change.
- Interest rate risk, the risk that interest rates will change.
- Currency risk, the risk that foreign exchange rates will change.
- Commodity risk, the risk that commodity prices (e.g. grains, metals) will change.

As with other forms of risk, _________ may be measured in a number of ways. Traditionally, this is done using a Value at Risk methodology. Value at risk is well established as a risk management technique, but it contains a number of limiting assumptions that constrain its accuracy.

a. Currency risk
b. Tracking error
c. Transaction risk
d. Market risk

34. The _________ is a term coined by economists Rajnish Mehra and Edward C. Prescott. It is based on the observation that in order to reconcile the much higher return on equity stock compared to government bonds in the United States, individuals must have implausibly high risk aversion according to standard economics models. Similar situations prevail in many other industrialized countries.

a. AAB
b. A Random Walk Down Wall Street
c. ABN Amro
d. Equity premium puzzle

35. In finance, the _________ is the difference between the quoted rates of return on two different investments, usually of different credit quality.

It is a compound of yield and spread.

The '_________ of X over Y' is simply the percentage return on investment (ROI) from financial instrument X minus the percentage return on investment from financial instrument Y (per annum.)

a. Debtor-in-possession financing
b. Yield spread
c. Duty of loyalty
d. Portfolio insurance

36. _________, is when a company issues common stock or shares to the public for the first time. They are often issued by smaller, younger companies seeking capital to expand, but can also be done by large privately-owned companies looking to become publicly traded.

In an _________ the issuer may obtain the assistance of an underwriting firm, which helps it determine what type of security to issue (common or preferred), best offering price and time to bring it to market.

a. Asian Financial Crisis
b. Insolvency
c. Initial public offering
d. Interest

1. In finance, _________ refers to the way a corporation finances its assets through some combination of equity, debt, or hybrid securities. A firm's _________ is then the composition or 'structure' of its liabilities. For example, a firm that sells $20 billion in equity and $80 billion in debt is said to be 20% equity-financed and 80% debt-financed.

a. Market for corporate control
b. Rights issue
c. Book building
d. Capital structure

2. In finance, _________ (or gearing) is borrowing money to supplement existing funds for investment in such a way that the potential positive or negative outcome is magnified and/or enhanced. It generally refers to using borrowed funds, or debt, so as to attempt to increase the returns to equity. Deleveraging is the action of reducing borrowings.

a. Pension fund
b. Financial endowment
c. Leverage
d. Limited partnership

3. An _________ is an economic concept that relates to the cost incurred by an entity (such as organizations) associated with problems such as divergent management-shareholder objectives and information asymmetry. The costs consist of two main sources:

1. The costs inherently associated with using an agent (e.g., the risk that agents will use organizational resource for their own benefit) and
2. The costs of techniques used to mitigate the problems associated with using an agent (e.g., the costs of producing financial statements or the use of stock options to align executive interests to shareholder interests.)

Though effects of _________ are present in any agency relationship, the term is most used in business contexts.

The information asymmetry that exists between shareholders and the Chief Executive Officer is generally considered to be a classic example of a principal-agent problem. The agent (the manager) is working on behalf of the principal (the shareholders), who does not observe the actions of the agent.

a. AAB
b. ABN Amro
c. A Random Walk Down Wall Street
d. Agency cost

4. In economics, business, and accounting, a _________ is the value of money that has been used up to produce something, and hence is not available for use anymore. In business, the _________ may be one of acquisition, in which case the amount of money expended to acquire it is counted as _________. In this case, money is the input that is gone in order to acquire the thing.

a. Marginal cost
b. Cost
c. Sliding scale fees
d. Fixed costs

5. _________ are business expenses that are not dependent on the level of production or sales. They tend to be time-related, such as salaries or rents being paid per month. This is in contrast to Variable costs, which are volume-related (and are paid per quantity.)
a. Marginal cost
b. Fixed costs
c. Transaction cost
d. Sliding scale fees

6. _________ are expenses that change in proportion to the activity of a business. In other words, _________ are the sum of marginal costs. It can also be considered normal costs. Along with fixed costs, _________ make up the two components of total cost. Direct Costs, however, are costs that can be associated with a particular cost object.
a. Cost accounting
b. Transaction cost
c. Variable costs
d. Fixed costs

7. The _________ is a measure of how revenue growth translates into growth in operating income. It is a measure of leverage, and of how risky (volatile) a company's operating income is.

There are various measures of _________, which can be interpreted analogously to financial leverage.

a. Asset turnover
b. Invested capital
c. Average accounting return
d. Operating leverage

8. In cost-volume-profit analysis, a form of management accounting, _________ is the marginal profit per unit sale. It is a useful quantity in carrying out various calculations, and can be used as a measure of operating leverage.

The Total _________ is Total Revenue (TR, or Sales) minus Total Variable Cost (TVC):

TContribution margin = TR >– TVC

The Unit _________ (C) is Unit Revenue (Price, P) minus Unit Variable Cost (V):

$C = P >- V$

The _________ Ratio is the percentage of Contribution over Total Revenue, which can be calculated from the unit contribution over unit price or total contribution over Total Revenue:

>

For instance, if the price is $10 and the unit variable cost is $2, then the unit _________ is $8, and the _________ ratio is $8/ $10 = 80%.

a. Contribution margin
b. 4-4-5 Calendar
c. 529 plan
d. 7-Eleven

9. In finance, a _________ is collateral that the holder of a position in securities, options, or futures contracts has to deposit to cover the credit risk of his counterparty (most often his broker.) This risk can arise if the holder has done any of the following:

- borrowed cash from the counterparty to buy securities or options,
- sold securities or options short, or
- entered into a futures contract.

The collateral can be in the form of cash or securities, and it is deposited in a _________ account. On U.S. futures exchanges, '_________' was formally called performance bond.

_________ buying is buying securities with cash borrowed from a broker, using other securities as collateral.

a. Margin
b. Share
c. Credit
d. Procter ' Gamble

10. _________ is normally any risk associated with any form of financing.

Depending on the nature of the investment, the type of 'investment' risk will vary. High risk investments have greater potential rewards, but you may lose your money instead by taking the risk for more money.

a. Liquidating dividend
b. Stock market index option
c. Financial risk
d. Revaluation

11. The _________ is an expected return that the provider of capital plans to earn on their investment.

Capital (money) used for funding a business should earn returns for the capital providers who risk their capital. For an investment to be worthwhile, the expected return on capital must be greater than the _________.

a. 4-4-5 Calendar
b. Capital intensity
c. Weighted average cost of capital
d. Cost of capital

12. _________ is that which is owed; usually referencing assets owed, but the term can cover other obligations. In the case of assets, _________ is a means of using future purchasing power in the present before a summation has been earned. Some companies and corporations use _________ as a part of their overall corporate finance strategy.
a. Debt
b. Credit cycle
c. Partial Payment
d. Cross-collateralization

13. A _________ is a party (e.g. person, organization, company, or government) that has a claim to the services of a second party. The first party, in general, has provided some property or service to the second party under the assumption (usually enforced by contract) that the second party will return an equivalent property or service. The second party is frequently called a debtor or borrower.
a. NOPLAT
b. Redemption value
c. False billing
d. Creditor

14. _________ is a legally declared inability or impairment of ability of an individual or organization to pay their creditors. Creditors may file a _________ petition against a debtor ('involuntary _________') in an effort to recoup a portion of what they are owed or initiate a restructuring. In the majority of cases, however, _________ is initiated by the debtor (a 'voluntary _________' that is filed by the bankrupt individual or organization.)

a. 529 plan
b. Bankruptcy
c. Debt settlement
d. 4-4-5 Calendar

15. In law, _________ refers to the process by which a company (or part of a company) is brought to an end, and the assets and property of the company redistributed. _________ can also be referred to as winding-up or dissolution, although dissolution technically refers to the last stage of _________. The process of _________ also arises when customs, an authority or agency in a country responsible for collecting and safeguarding customs duties, determines the final computation or ascertainment of the duties or drawback accruing on an entry.
a. Liquidation
b. Debt settlement
c. 4-4-5 Calendar
d. 529 plan

16. The _________ is the rate that a company is expected to pay to finance its assets. WACC is the minimum return that a company must earn on existing asset base to satisfy its creditors, owners, and other providers of capital.

Companies raise money from a number of sources: common equity, preferred equity, straight debt, convertible debt, exchangeable debt, warrants, options, pension liabilities, executive stock options, governmental subsidies, and so on.

a. Cost of capital
b. Capital intensity
c. Weighted average cost of capital
d. 4-4-5 Calendar

17. In business and accounting, _________s are everything of value that is owned by a person or company. The balance sheet of a firm records the monetary value of the _________s owned by the firm. The two major _________ classes are tangible _________s and intangible _________s.
a. EBITDA
b. Income
c. Accounts payable
d. Asset

18. The institution most often referenced by the word '_________' is a public or publicly traded _________, the shares of which are traded on a public stock exchange (e.g., the New York Stock Exchange or Nasdaq in the United States) where shares of stock of _________s are bought and sold by and to the general public. Most of the largest businesses in the world are publicly traded _________s. However, the majority of _________s are said to be closely held, privately held or close _________s, meaning that no ready market exists for the trading of shares.

a. Federal Home Loan Mortgage Corporation
b. Corporation
c. Depository Trust Company
d. Protect

19. _________ is a term in Corporate Finance used to indicate a condition when promises to creditors of a company are broken or honored with difficulty. Sometimes _________ can lead to bankruptcy. _________ is usually associated with some costs to the company and these are known as Costs of _________.

a. Cashflow matching
b. Commercial paper
c. Capital structure
d. Financial distress

20. In economics and contract theory, _________ deals with the study of decisions in transactions where one party has more or better information than the other. This creates an imbalance of power in transactions which can sometimes cause the transactions to go awry. Examples of this problem are adverse selection and moral hazard.

a. Information asymmetry
b. ABN Amro
c. AAB
d. A Random Walk Down Wall Street

21. In corporate finance, _________ is a cash flow available for distribution among all the security holders of a company. They include equity holders, debt holders, preferred stock holders, convertible security holders, and so on.

Note that the first three lines above are calculated for you on the standard Statement of Cash Flows.

a. Forfaiting
b. Funding
c. Safety stock
d. Free cash flow

22. In the theory of firm's capital structure and financing decisions, the _________ or Pecking Order Model was developed by Stewart C. Myers and Nicolas Majluf in 1984. It states that companies prioritize their sources of financing (from internal financing to equity) according to the law of least effort, or of least resistance, preferring to raise equity as a financing means of last resort. Hence, internal funds are used first, and when that is depleted, debt is issued, and when it is not sensible to issue any more debt, equity is issued.

a. 4-4-5 Calendar
b. 529 plan
c. The Dogs of the Dow
d. Pecking order theory

23. _________ is the balance of the amounts of cash being received and paid by a business during a defined period of time, sometimes tied to a specific project. Measurement of _________ can be used

- to evaluate the state or performance of a business or project.
- to determine problems with liquidity. Being profitable does not necessarily mean being liquid. A company can fail because of a shortage of cash, even while profitable.
- to generate project rate of returns. The time of _________s into and out of projects are used as inputs to financial models such as internal rate of return, and net present value.
- to examine income or growth of a business when it is believed that accrual accounting concepts do not represent economic realities. Alternately, _________ can be used to 'validate' the net income generated by accrual accounting.

_________ as a generic term may be used differently depending on context, and certain _________ definitions may be adapted by analysts and users for their own uses. Common terms include operating _________ and free _________.

_________s can be classified into:

1. Operational _________s: Cash received or expended as a result of the company's core business activities.
2. Investment _________s: Cash received or expended through capital expenditure, investments or acquisitions.
3. Financing _________s: Cash received or expended as a result of financial activities, such as interests and dividends.

All three together - the net _________ - are necessary to reconcile the beginning cash balance to the ending cash balance. Loan draw downs or equity injections, that is just shifting of capital but no expenditure as such, are not considered in the net _________.

a. Shareholder value
b. Real option
c. Corporate finance
d. Cash flow

24. A _________ is a situation that involves losing one quality or aspect of something in return for gaining another quality or aspect. It implies a decision to be made with full comprehension of both the upside and downside of a particular choice.

In economics the term is expressed as opportunity cost, referring the most preferred alternative given up.

a. Capital outflow
b. Break-even point
c. Total revenue
d. Trade-off

25. The _________ of Capital Structure refers to the idea that a company chooses how much debt finance and how much equity finance to use by balancing the costs and benefits. The classical version of the hypothesis goes back to Kraus and Litzenberger who considered a balance between the dead-weight costs of bankruptcy and the tax saving benefits of debt. Often agency costs are also included in the balance.

a. Firm commitment
b. Rights issue
c. Financial distress
d. Trade-off theory

1. A _________ is a payment made by a corporation to its shareholder members. When a corporation earns a profit or surplus, that money can be put to two uses: it can either be re-invested in the business (called retained earnings), or it can be paid to the shareholders as a _________. Many corporations retain a portion of their earnings and pay the remainder as a _________.

   a. Dividend puzzle
   b. Special dividend
   c. Dividend yield
   d. Dividend

2. A _________ is an equity investment option offered directly from the underlying company. The investor does not receive quarterly dividends directly as cash; instead, the investor's dividends are directly reinvested in the underlying equity. It should be noted that the investor still must pay tax annually on his or her dividend income, whether it is received or reinvested.

   a. Dividend payout ratio
   b. Dividend puzzle
   c. Dividend decision
   d. Dividend reinvestment plan

3. _________ is a payment of a dividend to stockholders that exceeds the company's retained earnings. Once retained earnings is depleted, capital accounts such as additional paid-in capital are decreased to make up for the remaining dividend to be paid to stockholders. When a _________ occurs, it is considered to be a return of investment instead of profits.

   a. Stock market index option
   b. Revolving credit
   c. Securities offering
   d. Liquidating dividend

4. A _________ is a payment made by a company to its shareholders that is separate from the typical recurring dividend cycle, if any, for the company. The difference may be the result of the date of issue, the amount, the type of payment, or a combination of these factors.

   The amount of the dividend is declared special or significant in relation to the stock price. For this reason, the ex-dividend date is set one stock trading day after the payment date. The stock will trade on an ex-distribution basis, adjusted for the amount of the dividend paid one trading day after the payment date.

   a. Dividend imputation
   b. Dividend decision
   c. Dividend puzzle
   d. Special dividend

5. _________ are those dividends paid out in form of additional stock shares of the issuing corporation or other corporation They are usually issued in proportion to shares owned (for example for every 100 shares of stock owned, 5% stock dividend will yield 5 extra shares). If this payment involves the issue of new shares, this is very similar to a stock split in that it increases the total number of shares while lowering the price of each share and does not change the market capitalization or the total value of the shares held

a. Stock or scrip dividends
b. Database auditing
c. Time-based currency
d. The Hong Kong Securities Institute

6. In business and finance, a _________ (also referred to as equity _________) of stock means a _________ of ownership in a corporation (company.) In the plural, stocks is often used as a synonym for _________s especially in the United States, but it is less commonly used that way outside of North America.

In the United Kingdom, South Africa, and Australia, stock can also refer to completely different financial instruments such as government bonds or, less commonly, to all kinds of marketable securities.

a. Margin
b. Bucket shop
c. Procter ' Gamble
d. Share

7. In some countries, including the United States and the United Kingdom, corporations can buy back their own stock in a share repurchase, also known as a _________ or share buyback. There has been a meteoric rise in the use of share repurchases in the U.S. in the past twenty years, from $5b in 1980 to $349b in 2005. A share repurchase distributes cash to existing shareholders in exchange for a fraction of the firm's outstanding equity.

a. Stockholder
b. Common stock
c. Trading curb
d. Stock repurchase

8. A _________ or stock divide increases or decreases the number of shares in a public company. The price is adjusted such that the before and after market capitalization of the company remains the same and dilution does not occur. Options and warrants are included.

a. Contract for difference
b. Stop price
c. Stop order
d. Stock split

9. The institution most often referenced by the word '_________' is a public or publicly traded _________, the shares of which are traded on a public stock exchange (e.g., the New York Stock Exchange or Nasdaq in the United States) where shares of stock of _________s are bought and sold by and to the general public. Most of the largest businesses in the world are publicly traded _________s. However, the majority of _________s are said to be closely held, privately held or close _________s, meaning that no ready market exists for the trading of shares.

a. Federal Home Loan Mortgage Corporation
b. Depository Trust Company
c. Protect
d. Corporation

10. On a stock exchange, a _________ is the opposite of a stock split, i.e. a stock merge - a reduction in the number of shares and an accompanying increase in the share price. The ratio is also reversed: 1-for-2, 1-for-3 and so on.

There is a stigma attached to doing this so it is not initiated without very good reason.

a. Trade date
b. Correlation trading
c. Conglomerate merger
d. Reverse stock split

11. A _________ or reacquired stock is stock which is bought back by the issuing company, reducing the amount of outstanding stock on the open market ('open market' including insiders' holdings.)

Stock repurchases are often used as a tax-efficient method to put cash into shareholders' hands, rather than pay dividends. Sometimes, companies do this when they feel that their stock is undervalued on the open market.

a. Generally Accepted Accounting Principles
b. Current asset
c. Trial balance
d. Treasury stock

12. In accounting, _________ or *Carrying value* is the value of an asset according to its balance sheet account balance. For assets, the value is based on the original cost of the asset less any depreciation, amortization or impairment costs made against the asset. A company's _________ is its total assets minus intangible assets and liabilities.

a. Pro forma
b. Current liabilities
c. Retained earnings
d. Book value

13. _________ is money paid by a company (or allied company or individual) to acquire its own shares of stock from a shareholder who is threatening to take control of, or unwanted influence of, the company.

The term is a neologism combining the terms greenback and blackmail, invented by journalists and commentators who saw the practices of corporate raiders as a form of blackmail. The target company is financially held hostage, and is legally forced to pay the _________er to go away.

a. 4-4-5 Calendar
b. Stock swap
c. 529 plan
d. Greenmail

14. _________ is a corporate finance term denoting a type of takeover bid. The _________ is a public, open offer or invitation (usually announced in a newspaper advertisement) by a prospective acquirer to all stockholders of a publicly traded corporation (the target corporation) to tender their stock for sale at a specified price during a specified time, subject to the tendering of a minimum and maximum number of shares. In a _________, the bidder contacts shareholders directly; the directors of the company may or may not have endorsed the _________ proposal.

a. Tender offer
b. Shareholder value
c. Follow-on offering
d. Cash is king

15. The key date to remember for dividend paying stocks is the _________. The _________ is different from the record date. The _________ is typically two trading days before the record date.

In order to receive the upcoming dividend payment payout, you must already own or you must purchase the stock prior to the _________. It is important to note that in most countries, when you buy or sell any stock, there is a three trading-day settlement period on your order.

a. Asian Financial Crisis
b. Index number
c. Insolvency
d. Ex-dividend date

16. The _________ is a stock exchange based in New York City, New York. It is the largest stock exchange in the world by dollar value of its listed companies securities. As of October 2008, the combined capitalization of all domestic _________ listed companies was $10.1 trillion.

a. 4-4-5 Calendar
b. 529 plan
c. New York Stock Exchange
d. 7-Eleven

17. A _________, securities exchange or (in Europe) bourse is a corporation or mutual organization which provides 'trading' facilities for stock brokers and traders, to trade stocks and other securities. _________s also provide facilities for the issue and redemption of securities as well as other financial instruments and capital events including the payment of income and dividends. The securities traded on a _________ include: shares issued by companies, unit trusts and other pooled investment products and bonds.
a. 7-Eleven
b. 4-4-5 Calendar
c. 529 plan
d. Stock Exchange

18. A mutual shareholder or _________ is an individual or company (including a corporation) that legally owns one or more shares of stock in a joint stock company. A company's shareholders collectively own that company. Thus, the typical goal of such companies is to enhance shareholder value.
a. Limit order
b. Trading curb
c. Stock market bubble
d. Stockholder

19. _________ is the imposition of two or more taxes on the same income (in the case of income taxes), asset (in the case of capital taxes), or financial transaction (in the case of sales taxes.) It refers to two distinct situations:

- taxation of dividend income without relief or credit for taxes paid by the company paying the dividend on the income from which the dividend is paid. This arises in the so-called 'classical' system of corporate taxation, used in the United States.
- taxation by two or more countries of the same income, asset or transaction, for example income paid by an entity of one country to a resident of a different country. The double liability is often mitigated by tax treaties between countries.

It is not unusual for a business or individual who is resident in one country to make a taxable gain (earnings, profits) in another. This person may find that he is obliged by domestic laws to pay tax on that gain locally and pay again in the country in which the gain was made. Since this is inequitable, many nations make bilateral _________ agreements with each other.

a. 7-Eleven
b. Double taxation
c. 4-4-5 Calendar
d. 529 plan

20. In finance, _________ refers to the way a corporation finances its assets through some combination of equity, debt, or hybrid securities. A firm's _________ is then the composition or 'structure' of its liabilities. For example, a firm that sells $20 billion in equity and $80 billion in debt is said to be 20% equity-financed and 80% debt-financed.

a. Rights issue
b. Market for corporate control
c. Book building
d. Capital structure

21. A _________ is a profit that results from investments into a capital asset, such as stocks, bonds or real estate, which exceeds the purchase price. It is the difference between a higher selling price and a lower purchase price, resulting in a financial gain for the seller. Conversely, a capital loss arises if the proceeds from the sale of a capital asset are less than the purchase price.

a. Payroll tax
b. Capital gains tax
c. Capital gain
d. Tax brackets

22. _________, is when a company issues common stock or shares to the public for the first time. They are often issued by smaller, younger companies seeking capital to expand, but can also be done by large privately-owned companies looking to become publicly traded.

In an _________ the issuer may obtain the assistance of an underwriting firm, which helps it determine what type of security to issue (common or preferred), best offering price and time to bring it to market.

a. Insolvency
b. Interest
c. Asian Financial Crisis
d. Initial public offering

23. In accounting, _________ refers to the portion of net income which is retained by the corporation rather than distributed to its owners as dividends. Similarly, if the corporation makes a loss, then that loss is retained and called variously retained losses, accumulated losses or accumulated deficit. _________ and losses are cumulative from year to year with losses offsetting earnings.

a. Matching principle
b. Retained earnings
c. Generally Accepted Accounting Principles
d. Historical cost

24. In economics, business, and accounting, a _________ is the value of money that has been used up to produce something, and hence is not available for use anymore. In business, the _________ may be one of acquisition, in which case the amount of money expended to acquire it is counted as _________. In this case, money is the input that is gone in order to acquire the thing.
a. Sliding scale fees
b. Cost
c. Marginal cost
d. Fixed costs

25. _________ represents the impact on the stock price that investors would cause in reaction to a change in policy of a company.
a. Volatility clustering
b. Bonus share
c. Trade date
d. Clientele effect

26. The _________ is the rate that a company is expected to pay to finance its assets. WACC is the minimum return that a company must earn on existing asset base to satisfy its creditors, owners, and other providers of capital.

Companies raise money from a number of sources: common equity, preferred equity, straight debt, convertible debt, exchangeable debt, warrants, options, pension liabilities, executive stock options, governmental subsidies, and so on.

a. Weighted average cost of capital
b. Cost of capital
c. 4-4-5 Calendar
d. Capital intensity

27. _________ or net present worth (NPW) is defined as the total present value (PV) of a time series of cash flows. It is a standard method for using the time value of money to appraise long-term projects. Used for capital budgeting, and widely throughout economics, it measures the excess or shortfall of cash flows, in present value terms, once financing charges are met.

a. Net present value
b. Tax shield
c. Negative gearing
d. Present value of costs

28. _________ is the planning process used to determine whether a firm's long term investments such as new machinery, replacement machinery, new plants, new products, and research development projects are worth pursuing. It is budget for major capital, or investment, expenditures.

Many formal methods are used in _________, including the techniques such as

- Net present value
- Profitability index
- Internal rate of return
- Modified Internal Rate of Return
- Equivalent annuity

These methods use the incremental cash flows from each potential investment, or project. Techniques based on accounting earnings and accounting rules are sometimes used - though economists consider this to be improper - such as the accounting rate of return, and 'return on investment.' Simplified and hybrid methods are used as well, such as payback period and discounted payback period.

a. Preferred stock
b. Capital budgeting
c. Shareholder value
d. Financial distress

29. _________ is the value on a given date of a future payment or series of future payments, discounted to reflect the time value of money and other factors such as investment risk. _________ calculations are widely used in business and economics to provide a means to compare cash flows at different times on a meaningful 'like to like' basis.

The most commonly applied model of the time value of money is compound interest.

a. Present value of benefits
b. Net present value
c. Present value
d. Negative gearing

30. _________ is the fraction of net income a firm pays to its stockholders in dividends:

>

The part of the earnings not paid to investors is left for investment to provide for future earnings growth. Investors seeking high current income and limited capital growth prefer companies with high _________. However investors seeking capital growth may prefer lower payout ratio because capital gains are taxed at a lower rate.

a. Dividend imputation
b. Dividend payout ratio
c. Dividend puzzle
d. Dividend yield

31. In finance, _________ is the process of estimating the potential market value of a financial asset or liability. they can be done on assets (for example, investments in marketable securities such as stocks, options, business enterprises, or intangible assets such as patents and trademarks) or on liabilities (e.g., Bonds issued by a company.) _________s are required in many contexts including investment analysis, capital budgeting, merger and acquisition transactions, financial reporting, taxable events to determine the proper tax liability, and in litigation.

a. Share
b. Procter ' Gamble
c. Margin
d. Valuation

1. _________ is a financial metric which represents operating liquidity available to a business. Along with fixed assets such as plant and equipment, _________ is considered a part of operating capital. It is calculated as current assets minus current liabilities.

a. Working capital
b. Working capital management
c. 4-4-5 Calendar
d. 529 plan

2. Decisions relating to working capital and short term financing are referred to as _________. These involve managing the relationship between a firm's short-term assets and its short-term liabilities. The goal of _________ is to ensure that the firm is able to continue its operations and that it has sufficient cash flow to satisfy both maturing short-term debt and upcoming operational expenses.

a. Working capital
b. Working capital management
c. 529 plan
d. 4-4-5 Calendar

3. _________, in bookkeeping, refers to assets, liabilities, income, and expenses recorded on individual pages of the so called book of final entry or ledger. Changes in _________ value are made by chronologically posting debit (DR) and credit (CR) entries to its page. Examples of _________s are cash, _________s receivable, mortgages, loans, land and buildings, common stock, sales, services provided, wages, and payroll overhead.

a. Alpha
b. Option
c. Accretion
d. Account

4. _________ is a file or account that contains money that a person or company owes to suppliers, but hasn't paid yet (a form of debt.) When you receive an invoice you add it to the file, and then you remove it when you pay. Thus, the A/P is a form of credit that suppliers offer to their purchasers by allowing them to pay for a product or service after it has already been received.

a. Outstanding balance
b. Accrual
c. Earnings before interest, taxes, depreciation and amortization
d. Accounts payable

5. _________ is a measure of the ability of a debtor to pay their debts as and when they fall due. It is usually expressed as a ratio or a percentage of current liabilities.

For a corporation with a published balance sheet there are various ratios used to calculate a measure of liquidity.

a. Operating profit margin
b. Invested capital
c. Operating leverage
d. Accounting liquidity

6. In business and accounting, _________s are everything of value that is owned by a person or company. The balance sheet of a firm records the monetary value of the _________s owned by the firm. The two major _________ classes are tangible _________s and intangible _________s.

a. Asset
b. Accounts payable
c. Income
d. EBITDA

7. _________ is a legally declared inability or impairment of ability of an individual or organization to pay their creditors. Creditors may file a _________ petition against a debtor ('involuntary _________') in an effort to recoup a portion of what they are owed or initiate a restructuring. In the majority of cases, however, _________ is initiated by the debtor (a 'voluntary _________' that is filed by the bankrupt individual or organization.)

a. Debt settlement
b. 4-4-5 Calendar
c. 529 plan
d. Bankruptcy

8. _________ is the balance of the amounts of cash being received and paid by a business during a defined period of time, sometimes tied to a specific project. Measurement of _________ can be used

- to evaluate the state or performance of a business or project.
- to determine problems with liquidity. Being profitable does not necessarily mean being liquid. A company can fail because of a shortage of cash, even while profitable.
- to generate project rate of returns. The time of _________s into and out of projects are used as inputs to financial models such as internal rate of return, and net present value.
- to examine income or growth of a business when it is believed that accrual accounting concepts do not represent economic realities. Alternately, _________ can be used to 'validate' the net income generated by accrual accounting.

_________ as a generic term may be used differently depending on context, and certain _________ definitions may be adapted by analysts and users for their own uses. Common terms include operating _________ and free _________.

_________s can be classified into:

1. Operational _________s: Cash received or expended as a result of the company's core business activities.
2. Investment _________s: Cash received or expended through capital expenditure, investments or acquisitions.
3. Financing _________s: Cash received or expended as a result of financial activities, such as interests and dividends.

All three together - the net _________ - are necessary to reconcile the beginning cash balance to the ending cash balance. Loan draw downs or equity injections, that is just shifting of capital but no expenditure as such, are not considered in the net _________.

a. Shareholder value
b. Real option
c. Cash flow
d. Corporate finance

9. _________ is a list for goods and materials held available in stock by a business. It is also used for a list of the contents of a household and for a list for testamentary purposes of the possessions of someone who has died. In accounting _________ is considered an asset.

a. A Random Walk Down Wall Street
b. AAB
c. ABN Amro
d. Inventory

10. In economics, the concept of the _________ refers to the decision-making time frame of a firm in which at least one factor of production is fixed. Costs which are fixed in the _________ have no impact on a firms decisions. For example a firm can raise output by increasing the amount of labour through overtime.

a. 529 plan
b. 4-4-5 Calendar
c. Long-run
d. Short-run

11. A _________ is an exchange of promises between two or more parties to do an act which is enforceable in a court of law. It is where an unqualified offer meets a qualified acceptance and the parties reach Consensus ad Idem. The parties must have the necessary capacity to _________ and the _________ must not be either trifling, indeterminate, impossible or illegal.

a. Contract
b. 7-Eleven
c. 4-4-5 Calendar
d. 529 plan

12. In economics, business, and accounting, a _________ is the value of money that has been used up to produce something, and hence is not available for use anymore. In business, the _________ may be one of acquisition, in which case the amount of money expended to acquire it is counted as _________. In this case, money is the input that is gone in order to acquire the thing.
a. Cost
b. Sliding scale fees
c. Fixed costs
d. Marginal cost

13. _________ is that which is owed; usually referencing assets owed, but the term can cover other obligations. In the case of assets, _________ is a means of using future purchasing power in the present before a summation has been earned. Some companies and corporations use _________ as a part of their overall corporate finance strategy.
a. Debt
b. Credit cycle
c. Cross-collateralization
d. Partial Payment

14. A _________ is any credit facility extended to a business by a bank or financial institution. A _________ may take several forms such as cash credit, overdraft, demand loan, export packing credit, term loan, discounting or purchase of commercial bills etc. It is like an account that can readily be tapped into if the need arises or not touched at all and saved for emergencies.
a. Debt-snowball method
b. Cash credit
c. Default Notice
d. Line of credit

15. _________ is the provision of resources (such as granting a loan) by one party to another party where that second party does not reimburse the first party immediately, thereby generating a debt, and instead arranges either to repay or return those resources (or material(s) of equal value) at a later date. The first party is called a creditor, also known as a lender, while the second party is called a debtor, also known as a borrower.

Movements of financial capital are normally dependent on either _________ or equity transfers.

a. Comparable
b. Clearing house
c. Credit
d. Warrant

16. _________ is one of a series of accounting transactions dealing with the billing of customers who owe money to a person, company or organization for goods and services that have been provided to the customer. In most business entities this is typically done by generating an invoice and mailing or electronically delivering it to the customer, who in turn must pay it within an established timeframe called credit or payment terms.

An example of a common payment term is Net 30, meaning payment is due in the amount of the invoice 30 days from the date of invoice.

a. Accounting methods
b. Accounts receivable
c. Income
d. Impaired asset

17. _________ is one of the accounting liquidity ratios, a financial ratio. This ratio measures the number of times, on average, receivables (e.g. Accounts Receivable) are collected during the period. A popular variant of the _________ is to convert it into an Average Collection Period in terms of days.

a. PEG ratio
b. Receivables turnover ratio
c. Return on equity
d. Sharpe ratio

18. The _________ is a financial ratio that measures whether or not a firm has enough resources to pay its debts over the next 12 months. It compares a firm's current assets to its current liabilities. It is expressed as follows:

$$\text{Current ratio} = \frac{\text{Current Assets}}{\text{Current Liabilities}}$$

For example, if WXY Company's current assets are $50,000,000 and its current liabilities are $40,000,000, then its _________ would be $50,000,000 divided by $40,000,000, which equals 1.25.

a. PEG ratio
b. Sustainable growth rate
c. Debt service coverage ratio
d. Current ratio

19. In finance, the Acid-test or _________ or liquid ratio measures the ability of a company to use its near cash or quick assets to immediately extinguish or retire its current liabilities. Quick assets include those current assets that presumably can be quickly converted to cash at close to their book values.

>

Generally, the acid test ratio should be 1:1 or better, however this varies widely by industry.

a. P/E ratio
b. Quick ratio
c. Financial ratio
d. Net assets

20. The _________ is the rate that a company is expected to pay to finance its assets. WACC is the minimum return that a company must earn on existing asset base to satisfy its creditors, owners, and other providers of capital.

Companies raise money from a number of sources: common equity, preferred equity, straight debt, convertible debt, exchangeable debt, warrants, options, pension liabilities, executive stock options, governmental subsidies, and so on.

a. 4-4-5 Calendar
b. Weighted average cost of capital
c. Cost of capital
d. Capital intensity

21. In finance, the term _________ describes the amount in cash that returns to the owners of a security. Normally it does not include the price variations, at the difference of the total return. _________ applies to various stated rates of return on stocks (common and preferred, and convertible), fixed income instruments (bonds, notes, bills, strips, zero coupon), and some other investment type insurance products (e.g. annuities.)

a. Macaulay duration
b. 4-4-5 Calendar
c. Yield to maturity
d. Yield

22. In finance, a _________ is a debt security, in which the authorized issuer owes the holders a debt and, depending on the terms of the _________, is obliged to pay interest (the coupon) and/or to repay the principal at a later date, termed maturity.

Thus a _________ is a loan: the issuer is the borrower, the _________ holder is the lender, and the coupon is the interest. _________s provide the borrower with external funds to finance long-term investments, or, in the case of government _________s, to finance current expenditure.

a. Bond
b. Puttable bond
c. Catastrophe bonds
d. Convertible bond

23. The _________ for an investment is a calculated annual yield for an investment, which may not pay out yearly. This allows investments which payout with different frequencies to be compared.
a. 529 plan
b. 4-4-5 Calendar
c. 7-Eleven
d. Bond equivalent yield

24. A '_________' is a 'Charge' that is paid to obtain the right to delay a payment. Essentially, the payer purchases the right to make a given payment in the future instead of in the Present. The '_________', or 'Charge' that must be paid to delay the payment, is simply the difference between what the payment amount would be if it were paid in the present and what the payment amount would be paid if it were paid in the future.
a. Risk aversion
b. Risk modeling
c. Value at risk
d. Discount

25. In finance, the _________ is the global financial market for short-term borrowing and lending. It provides short-term liquidity funding for the global financial system. The _________ is where short-term obligations such as Treasury bills, commercial paper and bankers' acceptances are bought and sold.

a. Consumer debt
b. Money market
c. Cramdown
d. Debt-for-equity swap

26. _________ is a fee paid on borrowed assets. It is the price paid for the use of borrowed money , or, money earned by deposited funds . Assets that are sometimes lent with _________ include money, shares, consumer goods through hire purchase, major assets such as aircraft, and even entire factories in finance lease arrangements.
a. Interest
b. A Random Walk Down Wall Street
c. Insolvency
d. AAB

27. Depending on the nature of the investment, the type of _________ will vary.

A common concern with any investment is that you may lose the money you invest - your capital. This risk is therefore often referred to as 'capital risk.'

If the assets you invest in are held in another currency there is a risk that currency movements alone may affect the value.

a. A Random Walk Down Wall Street
b. Investment risk
c. AAB
d. ABN Amro

28. An _________ is any government regulation or law that encourages or discourages foreign investment in the local economy, e.g. currency exchange limits.

As globalization integrates the economies of neighboring and of trading states, they are typically forced to trade off such rules as part of a common tax, tariff and trade regime, e.g. as defined by a free trade pact. _________ favoring local investors over global ones is typically discouraged in such pacts, and the idea of a separate _________ rapidly becomes a fiction or fantasy, as real decisions reflect the real need for nations to compete for investment, even from their own local investors.

a. AAB
b. Investment policy
c. A Random Walk Down Wall Street
d. ABN Amro

29. In finance, the _________ is used to determine a theoretically appropriate required rate of return of an asset, if that asset is to be added to an already well-diversified portfolio, given that asset's non-diversifiable risk. The model takes into account the asset's sensitivity to non-diversifiable risk (also known as systemic risk or market risk), often represented by the quantity beta (β) in the financial industry, as well as the expected return of the market and the expected return of a theoretical risk-free asset.

The model was introduced by Jack Treynor (1961, 1962), William Sharpe (1964), John Lintner (1965a,b) and Jan Mossin (1966) independently, building on the earlier work of Harry Markowitz on diversification and modern portfolio theory.

a. Random walk hypothesis
b. Hull-White model
c. Capital asset pricing model
d. Cox-Ingersoll-Ross model

30. Collect on Delivery or _________ is a financial transaction where the payment of products and/or services received is done at the time of actual delivery rather than paid for in advance. The term is mainly applied to products purchased from a third party, and payment is made to the deliverer.

This type of transaction was previously known better as '_________', however as other forms of payment became more common the word 'cash' was replaced with the word 'collect' to incorporate transactions with checks, credit cards or debit cards.

a. Channel stuffing
b. Net operating profit after tax
c. Treynor ratio
d. Cash on delivery

31. The phrase _________ refers to the aspect of corporate strategy, corporate finance and management dealing with the buying, selling and combining of different companies that can aid, finance, or help a growing company in a given industry grow rapidly without having to create another business entity.

An acquisition, also known as a takeover, is the buying of one company (the 'target') by another. An acquisition may be friendly or hostile.

a. Mergers and acquisitions
b. 4-4-5 Calendar
c. 7-Eleven
d. 529 plan

32. _________ is a type of credit that does not have a fixed number of payments, in contrast to installment credit. Examples of _________s used by consumers include credit cards. Corporate _________ facilities are typically used to provide liquidity for a company's day-to-day operations.

a. Commercial finance
b. Reverse stock split
c. Package loan
d. Revolving credit

33. In banking and finance, _________ denotes all activities from the time a commitment is made for a transaction until it is settled. _________ is necessary because the speed of trades is much faster than the cycle time for completing the underlying transaction.

In its widest sense _________ involves the management of post-trading, pre-settlement credit exposures, to ensure that trades are settled in accordance with market rules, even if a buyer or seller should become insolvent prior to settlement.

a. Clearing house
b. Share
c. Procter ' Gamble
d. Clearing

34. A _________ is a financial services company that provides clearing and settlement services for financial transactions, usually on a futures exchange, and often acts as central counterparty (the payor actually pays the _________, which then pays the payee). A _________ may also offer novation, the substitution of a new contract or debt for an old, or other credit enhancement services to its members.

The term is also used for banks like Suffolk Bank that acted as a restraint on the over-issuance of private bank notes.

a. Warrant
b. Valuation
c. Bucket shop
d. Clearing House

35. _________ refers to the computer-based systems used to perform financial transactions electronically.

The term is used for a number of different concepts:

- Cardholder-initiated transactions, where a cardholder makes use of a payment card
- Direct deposit payroll payments for a business to its employees, possibly via a payroll services company
- Direct debit payments from customer to business, where the transaction is initiated by the business with customer permission
- Electronic bill payment in online banking, which may be delivered by _________ or paper check
- Transactions involving stored value of electronic money, possibly in a private currency
- Wire transfer via an international banking network (generally carries a higher fee)
- Electronic Benefit Transfer

Electronic funds transferPOS (short for _________ at Point of Sale) is an Australian and New Zealand electronic processing system for credit cards, debit cards and charge cards.

European banks and card companies also sometimes reference 'Electronic funds transferPOS' as the system used for processing card transactions through terminals on points of sale, though the system is not the trademarked Australian/New Zealand variant.

Credit cards

_________ may be initiated by a cardholder when a payment card such as a credit card or debit card is used.

a. AAB
b. Electronic funds transfer
c. ABN Amro
d. A Random Walk Down Wall Street

36. The free _________ of a public company is an estimate of the proportion of shares that are not held by large owners and that are not stock with sales restrictions (restricted stock that cannot be sold until they become unrestricted stock.)

The free _________ or a public _________ is usually defined as being all shares held by investors other than:

- shares held by owners owning more than 5% of all shares (those could be institutional investors, 'strategic shareholders,' founders, executives, and other insiders' holdings)
- restricted stocks (granted to executives that can be, but don't have to be, registered insiders)
- insider holdings (it is assumed that insiders hold stock for the very long term)

The free _________ is an important criterion in quoting a share on the stock market.

To _________ a company means to list its shares on a public stock exchange through an initial public offering (or 'flotation'.)

- Open market
- Outstanding shares
- Market capitalization
- Public _________ *loat*
- Reverse takeover

.

a. Synthetic CDO
b. Trade finance
c. Float
d. Golden parachute

37. _________ consists of the sale of goods or merchandise from a fixed location, such as a department store, boutique or kiosk in small or individual lots for direct consumption by the purchaser. _________ may include subordinated services, such as delivery. Purchasers may be individuals or businesses.

a. Retailing
b. 4-4-5 Calendar
c. 7-Eleven
d. 529 plan

38. _________ is the transfer of funds from diverse accounts into a central account to improve the efficiency of cash management. The consolidation of cash into a single account allows a company to maintain smaller cash balances overall, and to identify excess cash available for short term investments. The cash available in different bank accounts are pooled into a master account.The advantages of _________ are 1) Cash control 2) Cash visibility .

a. Capitalization rate
b. Profitability index
c. Conditional prepayment rate
d. Cash concentration

39. In business and finance, a _________ (also referred to as equity _________) of stock means a _________ of ownership in a corporation (company.) In the plural, stocks is often used as a synonym for _________s especially in the United States, but it is less commonly used that way outside of North America.

In the United Kingdom, South Africa, and Australia, stock can also refer to completely different financial instruments such as government bonds or, less commonly, to all kinds of marketable securities.

a. Margin
b. Share
c. Bucket shop
d. Procter ' Gamble

40. _________ is an inventory strategy implemented to improve the return on investment of a business by reducing in-process inventory and its associated carrying costs. In order to achieve _________ the process must have signals of what is going on elsewhere within the process. This means that the process is often driven by a series of signals, which can be Kanban, that tell production processes when to make the next part.
a. Pac-Man defense
b. Just-in-time
c. Greed and fear
d. Debtor-in-possession financing

41. _________ is defined by APICS as a method for the effective planning of all resources of a manufacturing company. Ideally, it addresses operational planning in units, financial planning in dollars, and has a simulation capability to answer 'what-if' questions and extension of closed-loop _________. Manufacturing Resource Planning - Around 1980, over-frequent changes in sales forecasts, entailing continual readjustments in production, as well as the unsuitability of the parameters fixed by the system, led _________ to evolve into a new concept : _________.

This is not exclusively a software function, but a marriage of people skills, dedication to data base accuracy, and computer resources.

a. 7-Eleven
b. 529 plan
c. 4-4-5 Calendar
d. Manufacturing resource planning

42. _________ exists when one firm provides goods or services to a customer with an agreement to bill them later, or receive a shipment or service from a supplier under an agreement to pay them later. It can be viewed as an essential element of capitalization in an operating business because it can reduce the required capital investment to operate the business if it is managed properly. _________ is the largest use of capital for a majority of business to business (B2B) sellers in the United States and is a critical source of capital for a majority of all businesses.
a. 529 plan
b. 4-4-5 Calendar
c. Trade credit
d. Going concern

43. _________, consists of the buying and selling of products or services over electronic systems such as the Internet and other computer networks. The amount of trade conducted electronically has grown extraordinarily with widespread Internet usage. The use of commerce is conducted in this way, spurring and drawing on innovations in electronic funds transfer, supply chain management, Internet marketing, online transaction processing, electronic data interchange (EDI), inventory management systems, and automated data collection systems.

a. AAB
b. A Random Walk Down Wall Street
c. Electronic commerce
d. ABN Amro

44. _________ or financing is to provide capital (funds), which means money for a project, a person, a business or any other private or public institutions.

Those funds can be allocated for either short term or long term purposes. The health fund is a new way of _________ private healthcare centers.

a. Synthetic CDO
b. Product life cycle
c. Proxy fight
d. Funding

45. The _________ is a daily reference rate based on the interest rates at which banks borrow unsecured funds from banks in the London wholesale money market (or interbank market.) It is roughly comparable to the U.S. Federal funds rate.

During 1984 it became apparent that an increasing number of banks were trading actively in a variety of relatively new market instruments, notably interest rate swaps, foreign currency options and forward rate agreements.

a. Shanghai Interbank Offered Rate
b. Fixed interest
c. Risk-free interest rate
d. London Interbank Offered Rate

46. An _________ is a loan, often for a short term, secured by a company's assets. Real estate, A/R, inventory, and equipment are typical assets used to back the loan. The loan may be backed by a single category of assets or some combination of assets, for instance, a combination of A/R and equipment.

a. Amortizing loan
b. External financing
c. Asset-based loan
d. ASCOT

47. In law, a _________ is a form of security interest granted over an item of property to secure the payment of a debt or performance of some other obligation. The owner of the property, who grants the _________, is referred to as the lienor and the person who has the benefit of the _________ is referred to as the _________ee.

The etymological root is: Anglo-French _________, loyen bond, restraint, from Latin ligamen, from ligare to bind.

a. Joint venture
b. Family and Medical Leave Act
c. Sarbanes-Oxley Act
d. Lien

1. _________ refers to an assessment of the viability, stability and profitability of a business, sub-business or project.

It is performed by professionals who prepare reports using ratios that make use of information taken from financial statements and other reports. These reports are usually presented to top management as one of their bases in making business decisions.

a. Financial analysis
b. Value investing
c. 529 plan
d. 4-4-5 Calendar

2. _________ is the difference between price and the costs of bringing to market whatever it is that is accounted as an enterprise (whether by harvest, extraction, manufacture, or purchase) in terms of the component costs of delivered goods and/or services and any operating or other expenses.

A key difficulty in measuring profit is in defining costs. Pure economic monetary profits can be zero or negative even in competitive equilibrium when accounted monetized costs exceed monetized price.

a. A Random Walk Down Wall Street
b. Accounting profit
c. Economic profit
d. AAB

3. _________, Net Margin, Net _________ or Net Profit Ratio all refer to a measure of profitability. It is calculated using a formula and written as a percentage or a number.

$$\text{Net profit margin} = \frac{\text{Net profit after taxes}}{\text{Net Sales}}$$

The _________ is mostly used for internal comparison.

a. Net profit margin
b. Profit maximization
c. 4-4-5 Calendar
d. Profit margin

4. In finance, a _________ is collateral that the holder of a position in securities, options, or futures contracts has to deposit to cover the credit risk of his counterparty (most often his broker.) This risk can arise if the holder has done any of the following:

- borrowed cash from the counterparty to buy securities or options,
- sold securities or options short, or
- entered into a futures contract.

The collateral can be in the form of cash or securities, and it is deposited in a _________ account. On U.S. futures exchanges, '_________' was formally called performance bond.

_________ buying is buying securities with cash borrowed from a broker, using other securities as collateral.

a. Share
b. Procter ' Gamble
c. Credit
d. Margin

5. In financial accounting, a _________ or statement of financial position is a summary of a person's or organization's balances. Assets, liabilities and ownership equity are listed as of a specific date, such as the end of its financial year. A _________ is often described as a snapshot of a company's financial condition.
a. Statement of retained earnings
b. Statement on Auditing Standards No. 70: Service Organizations
c. Financial statements
d. Balance sheet

6. _________, refers to consumption opportunity gained by an entity within a specified time frame, which is generally expressed in monetary terms. However, for households and individuals, '_________ is the sum of all the wages, salaries, profits, interests payments, rents and other forms of earnings received... in a given period of time.' For firms, _________ generally refers to net-profit: what remains of revenue after expenses have been subtracted.
a. Accrual
b. Annual report
c. OIBDA
d. Income

7. An _________ is a financial statement for companies that indicates how Revenue is transformed into net income The purpose of the _________ is to show managers and investors whether the company made or lost money during the period being reported.

The important thing to remember about an _________ is that it represents a period of time.

a. AAB
b. A Random Walk Down Wall Street
c. ABN Amro
d. Income statement

8. In finance, a _________ or accounting ratio is a ratio of two selected numerical values taken from an enterprise's financial statements. There are many standard ratios used to try to evaluate the overall financial condition of a corporation or other organization. They may be used by managers within a firm, by current and potential shareholders (owners) of a firm, and by a firm's creditors. Security analysts use these to compare the strengths and weaknesses in various companies.
a. Price/cash flow ratio
b. Sustainable growth rate
c. Return on capital employed
d. Financial ratio

9. _________ is a measure of the ability of a debtor to pay their debts as and when they fall due. It is usually expressed as a ratio or a percentage of current liabilities.

For a corporation with a published balance sheet there are various ratios used to calculate a measure of liquidity.

a. Accounting liquidity
b. Invested capital
c. Operating leverage
d. Operating profit margin

10. In finance, _________ is the ability of an entity to pay its debts with available cash. _________ can also be described as the ability of a corporation to meet its long-term fixed expenses and to accomplish long-term expansion and growth. The better a company's _________, the better it is financially.
a. Mid price
b. Capital asset
c. Political risk
d. Solvency

11. _________ is a list for goods and materials held available in stock by a business. It is also used for a list of the contents of a household and for a list for testamentary purposes of the possessions of someone who has died. In accounting _________ is considered an asset.

a. ABN Amro
b. Inventory
c. A Random Walk Down Wall Street
d. AAB

12. The _________ is an equation that equals the cost of goods sold divided by the average inventory. Average inventory equals beginning inventory plus ending inventory divided by 2.

The formula for _________:

$$\text{Inventory Turnover} = \frac{\text{Cost of Goods Sold}}{\text{Average Inventory}}$$

The formula for average inventory:

$$\text{Average Inventory} = \frac{\text{Beginning inventory+Ending inventory}}{2}$$

A low turnover rate may point to overstocking, obsolescence, or deficiencies in the product line or marketing effort.

a. Inventory turnover
b. Information ratio
c. Earnings yield
d. Operating leverage

13. _________ is a financial metric which represents operating liquidity available to a business. Along with fixed assets such as plant and equipment, _________ is considered a part of operating capital. It is calculated as current assets minus current liabilities.

a. Working capital
b. 529 plan
c. Working capital management
d. 4-4-5 Calendar

14. In business and accounting, _________s are everything of value that is owned by a person or company. The balance sheet of a firm records the monetary value of the _________s owned by the firm. The two major _________ classes are tangible _________s and intangible _________s.

a. EBITDA
b. Accounts payable
c. Income
d. Asset

15. _________ is a financial ratio that measures the efficiency of a company's use of its assets in generating sales revenue or sales income to the company.

$$Asset\ Turnover = \frac{Sales}{AverageTotalAssets}$$

- 'Sales' is the value of 'Net Sales' or 'Sales' from the company's income statement
- 'Average Total Assets' is the value of 'Total assets' from the company's balance sheet in the beginning and the end of the fiscal period divided by 2.

- Assets turnover

.

a. Earnings yield
b. Asset turnover
c. Inventory turnover
d. Average accounting return

16. In accounting, a _________ is an asset on the balance sheet which is expected to be sold or otherwise used up in the near future, usually within one year, or one business cycle - whichever is longer. Typical _________s include cash, cash equivalents, accounts receivable, inventory, the portion of prepaid accounts which will be used within a year, and short-term investments.

On the balance sheet, assets will typically be classified into _________s and long-term assets.

a. Write-off
b. Current asset
c. Long-term liabilities
d. Historical cost

17. In accounting, _________ are considered liabilities of the business that are to be settled in cash within the fiscal year or the operating cycle, whichever period is longer.

For example accounts payable for goods, services or supplies that were purchased for use in the operation of the business and payable within a normal period of time would be _________.

Bonds, mortgages and loans that are payable over a term exceeding one year would be fixed liabilities.

a. Gross sales
b. Net income
c. Closing entries
d. Current liabilities

18. _________ is normally any risk associated with any form of financing.

Depending on the nature of the investment, the type of 'investment' risk will vary. High risk investments have greater potential rewards, but you may lose your money instead by taking the risk for more money.

a. Financial risk
b. Stock market index option
c. Revaluation
d. Liquidating dividend

19. The term _________ is a term applied to practices that are perfunctory, or seek to satisfy the minimum requirements or to conform to a convention or doctrine. It has different meanings in different fields.

In accounting, _________ earnings are those earnings of companies in addition to actual earnings calculated under the Generally Accepted Accounting Principles (GAAP) in their quarterly and yearly financial reports.

a. Deferred financing costs
b. Deferred income
c. Long-term liabilities
d. Pro forma

20. In accounting, _________ or *Carrying value* is the value of an asset according to its balance sheet account balance. For assets, the value is based on the original cost of the asset less any depreciation, amortization or impairment costs made against the asset. A company's _________ is its total assets minus intangible assets and liabilities.

a. Current liabilities
b. Retained earnings
c. Book value
d. Pro forma

21. In economic models, the _________ time frame assumes no fixed factors of production. Firms can enter or leave the marketplace, and the cost (and availability) of land, labor, raw materials, and capital goods can be assumed to vary. In contrast, in the short-run time frame, certain factors are assumed to be fixed, because there is not sufficient time for them to change.
a. Short-run
b. 4-4-5 Calendar
c. 529 plan
d. Long-run

22. _________ is the price at which an asset would trade in a competitive Walrasian auction setting. _________ is often used interchangeably with open _________, fair value or fair _________, although these terms have distinct definitions in different standards, and may differ in some circumstances.

International Valuation Standards defines _________ as 'the estimated amount for which a property should exchange on the date of valuation between a willing buyer and a willing seller in an arm'e;s-length transaction after proper marketing wherein the parties had each acted knowledgeably, prudently, and without compulsion.'

_________ is a concept distinct from market price, which is 'e;the price at which one can transact'e;, while _________ is 'e;the true underlying value'e; according to theoretical standards.

a. Wrap account
b. Market value
c. Debt restructuring
d. T-Model

23. In economics, business, and accounting, a _________ is the value of money that has been used up to produce something, and hence is not available for use anymore. In business, the _________ may be one of acquisition, in which case the amount of money expended to acquire it is counted as _________. In this case, money is the input that is gone in order to acquire the thing.
a. Fixed costs
b. Cost
c. Sliding scale fees
d. Marginal cost

24. The _________ is an expected return that the provider of capital plans to earn on their investment.

Capital (money) used for funding a business should earn returns for the capital providers who risk their capital. For an investment to be worthwhile, the expected return on capital must be greater than the _________.

a. 4-4-5 Calendar
b. Weighted average cost of capital
c. Capital intensity
d. Cost of capital

25. In finance, _________ (or gearing) is borrowing money to supplement existing funds for investment in such a way that the potential positive or negative outcome is magnified and/or enhanced. It generally refers to using borrowed funds, or debt, so as to attempt to increase the returns to equity. Deleveraging is the action of reducing borrowings.

a. Limited partnership
b. Financial endowment
c. Pension fund
d. Leverage

26. _________ is the balance of the amounts of cash being received and paid by a business during a defined period of time, sometimes tied to a specific project. Measurement of _________ can be used

- to evaluate the state or performance of a business or project.
- to determine problems with liquidity. Being profitable does not necessarily mean being liquid. A company can fail because of a shortage of cash, even while profitable.
- to generate project rate of returns. The time of _________s into and out of projects are used as inputs to financial models such as internal rate of return, and net present value.
- to examine income or growth of a business when it is believed that accrual accounting concepts do not represent economic realities. Alternately, _________ can be used to 'validate' the net income generated by accrual accounting.

_________ as a generic term may be used differently depending on context, and certain _________ definitions may be adapted by analysts and users for their own uses. Common terms include operating _________ and free _________.

_________s can be classified into:

1. Operational _________s: Cash received or expended as a result of the company's core business activities.
2. Investment _________s: Cash received or expended through capital expenditure, investments or acquisitions.
3. Financing _________s: Cash received or expended as a result of financial activities, such as interests and dividends.

All three together - the net _________ - are necessary to reconcile the beginning cash balance to the ending cash balance. Loan draw downs or equity injections, that is just shifting of capital but no expenditure as such, are not considered in the net _________.

a. Cash flow
b. Corporate finance
c. Shareholder value
d. Real option

27. _________ is a fee paid on borrowed assets. It is the price paid for the use of borrowed money , or, money earned by deposited funds . Assets that are sometimes lent with _________ include money, shares, consumer goods through hire purchase, major assets such as aircraft, and even entire factories in finance lease arrangements.

a. Interest
b. Insolvency
c. A Random Walk Down Wall Street
d. AAB

28. Times interest earned (TIE) or _________ is a measure of a company's ability to honor its debt payments. It may be calculated as either EBIT or EBITDA divided by the total interest payable.

$$\text{Times-Interest-Earned} = \frac{\text{EBIT or EBITDA}}{\text{Interest Charges}}$$

- Financial ratio
- Financial leverage
- EBIT
- EBITDA
- Debt service coverage ratio

Interest Charges = Traditionally 'charges' refers to interest expense found on the income statement.

Times Interest Earned or Interest Coverage is a great tool when measuring a company's ability to meet its debt obligations.

a. Interest coverage ratio
b. Assets turnover
c. Earnings per share
d. Information ratio

29. In accounting, _________ or sales profit is the difference between revenue and the cost of making a product or providing a service, before deducting overhead, payroll, taxation, and interest payments. Note that this is different than operating profit.

Net sales are calculated:

Net sales = Sales - Sales returns and allowances

_________ is found by deducting the cost of goods sold:

_________ = Net sales - Cost of goods sold

_________ should not be confused with net income:

Net income = _________ - Total operating expenses

Cost of goods sold is calculated differently for merchandising business than for a manufacturer.

a. Gross income
b. Cash flow
c. Real option
d. Gross profit

30. _________ is a financial ratio used to assess the profitability of a firm's core activities, excluding fixed costs.

The general calculation is

$$\text{Gross profit margin} = \frac{\text{Revenue} - \text{Cost of Sales}}{\text{Revenue}}$$

The _________ is related to the net profit margin, which assesses the profitability of an organization after including fixed costs.

Indicates the relationship between net sales revenue and the cost of goods sold.

a. Gross profit
b. Gross profit margin
c. Second lien loan
d. Tender offer

31. _________ is a measure of a company's earning power from ongoing operations, equal to earnings before the deduction of interest payments and income taxes.

To accountants, economic profit, or EP, is a single-period metric to determine the value created by a company in one period - usually a year. It is the net profit after tax less the equity charge, a risk-weighted cost of capital.

a. Economic profit
b. AAB
c. A Random Walk Down Wall Street
d. Operating profit

32. In business, operating margin, operating income margin, _________ or return on sales (ROS) is the ratio of operating income (operating profit in the UK) divided by net sales, usually presented in percent.

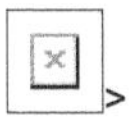

(Relevant figures in italics)

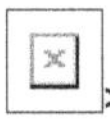

It is a measurement of what proportion of a company's revenue is left over, before taxes and other indirect costs (such as rent, bonus, interest, etc.), after paying for variable costs of production as wages, raw materials, etc. A good operating margin is needed for a company to be able to pay for its fixed costs, such as interest on debt.

a. Interest coverage ratio
b. Operating profit margin
c. Operating leverage
d. Average rate of return

33. In business and finance accounting, _________ is equal to the gross profit minus overheads minus interest payable plus/minus one off items for a given time period (usually: accounting period.)

A common synonym for '_________' when discussing financial statements (which include a balance sheet and an income statement) is the bottom line. This term results from the traditional appearance of an income statement which shows all allocated revenues and expenses over a specified time period with the resulting summation on the bottom line of the report.

a. Gross sales
b. Salvage value
c. Deferred
d. Net profit

34. Profit margin, net margin, _________ or net profit ratio all refer to a measure of profitability. It is calculated by finding the net profit as a percentage of the revenue.

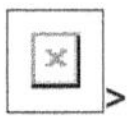

>

The profit margin is mostly used for internal comparison.

a. 4-4-5 Calendar
b. Profit maximization
c. Profit margin
d. Net profit margin

35. The _________ percentage shows how profitable a company's assets are in generating revenue.

_________ can be computed as:

$$\text{ROA} = \frac{\text{Net Income}}{\text{Total Assets}}$$

This number tells you 'what the company can do with what it's got', i.e. how many dollars of earnings they derive from each dollar of assets they control. It's a useful number for comparing competing companies in the same industry.

a. Return on Assets
b. Return on sales
c. P/E ratio
d. Receivables turnover ratio

36. _________ measures the rate of return on the ownership interest (shareholders' equity) of the common stock owners. _________ is viewed as one of the most important financial ratios. It measures a firm's efficiency at generating profits from every dollar of shareholders' equity (also known as net assets or assets minus liabilities.)

a. Return on equity
b. Return of capital
c. Diluted Earnings Per Share
d. Return on sales

37. An _________ is an economic concept that relates to the cost incurred by an entity (such as organizations) associated with problems such as divergent management-shareholder objectives and information asymmetry. The costs consist of two main sources:

1. The costs inherently associated with using an agent (e.g., the risk that agents will use organizational resource for their own benefit) and
2. The costs of techniques used to mitigate the problems associated with using an agent (e.g., the costs of producing financial statements or the use of stock options to align executive interests to shareholder interests.)

Though effects of _________ are present in any agency relationship, the term is most used in business contexts.

The information asymmetry that exists between shareholders and the Chief Executive Officer is generally considered to be a classic example of a principal-agent problem. The agent (the manager) is working on behalf of the principal (the shareholders), who does not observe the actions of the agent.

a. Agency cost
b. A Random Walk Down Wall Street
c. ABN Amro
d. AAB

38. _________ are costs incurred on the purchase of land, buildings, construction and equipment to be used in the production of goods or the rendering of services. In other words, the total cost needed to bring a project to a commercially operable status. However, _________ are not limited to the initial construction of a factory or other business.
a. Defined contribution plan
b. Trade-off
c. Capital outflow
d. Capital costs

39. _________ are the earnings returned on the initial investment amount.

In the US, the Financial Accounting Standards Board (FASB) requires companies' income statements to report _________ for each of the major categories of the income statement: continuing operations, discontinued operations, extraordinary items, and net income.

The _________ formula does not include preferred dividends for categories outside of continued operations and net income.

a. Inventory turnover
b. Earnings per share
c. Average accounting return
d. Assets turnover

40. The _________ of a stock is a measure of the price paid for a share relative to the annual income or profit earned by the firm per share. It is a financial ratio used for valuation: a higher _________ means that investors are paying more for each unit of income, so the stock is more expensive compared to one with lower _________.

The _________ has units of years, which can be interpreted as 'number of years of earnings to pay back purchase price'.

a. Return of capital
b. Quick ratio
c. Sustainable growth rate
d. P/E ratio

41. In business and finance, a _________ (also referred to as equity _________) of stock means a _________ of ownership in a corporation (company.) In the plural, stocks is often used as a synonym for _________s especially in the United States, but it is less commonly used that way outside of North America.

In the United Kingdom, South Africa, and Australia, stock can also refer to completely different financial instruments such as government bonds or, less commonly, to all kinds of marketable securities.

a. Bucket shop
b. Share
c. Procter ' Gamble
d. Margin

42. A _________ is a payment made by a corporation to its shareholder members. When a corporation earns a profit or surplus, that money can be put to two uses: it can either be re-invested in the business (called retained earnings), or it can be paid to the shareholders as a _________. Many corporations retain a portion of their earnings and pay the remainder as a _________.

a. Dividend yield
b. Special dividend
c. Dividend puzzle
d. Dividend

43. _________ is the fraction of net income a firm pays to its stockholders in dividends:

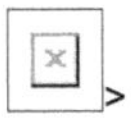
>

The part of the earnings not paid to investors is left for investment to provide for future earnings growth. Investors seeking high current income and limited capital growth prefer companies with high _________. However investors seeking capital growth may prefer lower payout ratio because capital gains are taxed at a lower rate.

a. Dividend puzzle
b. Dividend imputation
c. Dividend payout ratio
d. Dividend yield

44. _________s is a real estate appraisal term referring to properties with characteristics that are similar to a subject property whose value is being sought. This can be accomplished either by a real estate agent who attempts to establish the value of a potential client's home or property through market analysis or, by a licensed or certified appraiser or surveyor using more defined methods, when performing a real estate appraisal.

Five factors are usually considered when determining _________s:

- Conditions of Sale -- Did the _________ recently transact under conditions (e.g. -- arms length, distress sale, estate settlement) which are consistent with the standard of value under which the appraisal is being performed?
- Financing Conditions -- Was the _________ transaction influenced by non-market or other favorable (or even unfavorable) financing terms? For example, if the _________ sold with a below-market interest rate provided by the seller, and if the standard of value (e.g. -- market value) assumes no such abnormal financing, then the appraiser may need to adjust the _________ price by an amount equal to the estimated impact of the favorable financing.
- Market Conditions -- This is often referred to as the time adjustment and accounts for changing prices over time.
- Locational Comparability -- Are the _________ and the subject property influenced by the same locational characteristics? For example, even two houses in the same neighborhood may have different views which cause one to be more valuable than the other.
- Physical Comparability -- This includes such factors as size, condition, quality, and age.

A real estate appraisal is like any other statistical sampling process. The _________s are the samples drawn and measured, and the outcome is an estimate of value -- called an 'opinion of value' in the terminology of real estate appraisal.

a. Comparable
b. Bucket shop
c. Procter ' Gamble
d. Margin

45. The _________ is the rate that a company is expected to pay to finance its assets. WACC is the minimum return that a company must earn on existing asset base to satisfy its creditors, owners, and other providers of capital.

Companies raise money from a number of sources: common equity, preferred equity, straight debt, convertible debt, exchangeable debt, warrants, options, pension liabilities, executive stock options, governmental subsidies, and so on.

a. Cost of capital
b. 4-4-5 Calendar
c. Capital intensity
d. Weighted average cost of capital

46. In business, _________ is income that a company receives from its normal business activities, usually from the sale of goods and services to customers. Some companies also receive _________ from interest, dividends or royalties paid to them by other companies. _________ may refer to business income in general, or it may refer to the amount, in a monetary unit, received during a period of time, as in 'Last year, Company X had _________ of $32 million.'

In many countries, including the UK, _________ is referred to as turnover.

a. Matching principle
b. Bottom line
c. Furniture, Fixtures and Equipment
d. Revenue

1. The institution most often referenced by the word '_________' is a public or publicly traded _________, the shares of which are traded on a public stock exchange (e.g., the New York Stock Exchange or Nasdaq in the United States) where shares of stock of _________s are bought and sold by and to the general public. Most of the largest businesses in the world are publicly traded _________s. However, the majority of _________s are said to be closely held, privately held or close _________s, meaning that no ready market exists for the trading of shares.

a. Federal Home Loan Mortgage Corporation
b. Depository Trust Company
c. Protect
d. Corporation

2. The phrase _________ refers to the aspect of corporate strategy, corporate finance and management dealing with the buying, selling and combining of different companies that can aid, finance, or help a growing company in a given industry grow rapidly without having to create another business entity.

An acquisition, also known as a takeover, is the buying of one company (the 'target') by another. An acquisition may be friendly or hostile.

a. 7-Eleven
b. Mergers and acquisitions
c. 4-4-5 Calendar
d. 529 plan

3. _________ or amalgamation is the act of merging many things into one. In business, it often refers to the mergers or acquisitions of many smaller companies into much larger ones. The financial accounting term of _________ refers to the aggregated financial statements of a group company as consolidated account.

a. Retained earnings
b. Cost of goods sold
c. Write-off
d. Consolidation

4. In corporate finance, _________ is a cash flow available for distribution among all the security holders of a company. They include equity holders, debt holders, preferred stock holders, convertible security holders, and so on.

Note that the first three lines above are calculated for you on the standard Statement of Cash Flows.

a. Funding
b. Forfaiting
c. Safety stock
d. Free cash flow

5. In economics, a _________ is the combination of two or more firms competing in the same market with the same good or service.

a. Passive income
b. 4-4-5 Calendar
c. Fixed exchange rate system
d. Horizontal merger

6. A _________, in business matters, is an entity that is controlled by a bigger and more powerful entity. The controlled entity is called a company, corporation, or limited liability company, and the controlling entity is called its parent (or the parent company.) The reason for this distinction is that a lone company cannot be a _________ of any organization; only an entity representing a legal fiction as a separate entity can be a _________.

a. Joint stock company
b. 529 plan
c. 4-4-5 Calendar
d. Subsidiary

7. In business, a _________ is the purchase of one company (the target) by another (the acquirer or bidder). In the UK the term refers to the acquisition of a public company whose shares are listed on a stock exchange, in contrast to the acquisition of a private company.

Before a bidder makes an offer for another company, it usually first informs that company's board of directors.

a. 529 plan
b. 4-4-5 Calendar
c. Stock swap
d. Takeover

8. _________ is the balance of the amounts of cash being received and paid by a business during a defined period of time, sometimes tied to a specific project. Measurement of _________ can be used

- to evaluate the state or performance of a business or project.
- to determine problems with liquidity. Being profitable does not necessarily mean being liquid. A company can fail because of a shortage of cash, even while profitable.
- to generate project rate of returns. The time of _________s into and out of projects are used as inputs to financial models such as internal rate of return, and net present value.
- to examine income or growth of a business when it is believed that accrual accounting concepts do not represent economic realities. Alternately, _________ can be used to 'validate' the net income generated by accrual accounting.

_________ as a generic term may be used differently depending on context, and certain _________ definitions may be adapted by analysts and users for their own uses. Common terms include operating _________ and free _________.

_________s can be classified into:

1. Operational _________s: Cash received or expended as a result of the company's core business activities.
2. Investment _________s: Cash received or expended through capital expenditure, investments or acquisitions.
3. Financing _________s: Cash received or expended as a result of financial activities, such as interests and dividends.

All three together - the net _________ - are necessary to reconcile the beginning cash balance to the ending cash balance. Loan draw downs or equity injections, that is just shifting of capital but no expenditure as such, are not considered in the net _________.

a. Corporate finance
b. Cash flow
c. Shareholder value
d. Real option

9. A _________ is officially defined as being 'any merger that is not horizontal or vertical; in general, it is the combination of firms in different industries or firms operating in different geographic areas'. _________s can serve various purposes, including extending corporate territories and extending a product range. One example of a _________ was the merger between the Walt Disney Company and the American Broadcasting Company.

a. Conglomerate merger
b. Volatility clustering
c. Refunding
d. Redemption value

10. _________, in microeconomics, are the cost advantages that a business obtains due to expansion. _________ may be utilized by any size firm expanding its scale of operation.

a. Uniform Commercial Code
b. Articles of incorporation
c. Employee Retirement Income Security Act
d. Economies of scale

11. In finance, _________ is the process of business expansion due to increased output, sales, or both, as opposed to mergers, acquisitions the _________ rate also excludes the impact of foreign exchange. Growth including foreign exchange, but excluding divestitures and acquisitions is often referred to as core growth.

a. Organic growth
b. A Random Walk Down Wall Street
c. AAB
d. ABN Amro

12. In finance, _________ refers to the way a corporation finances its assets through some combination of equity, debt, or hybrid securities. A firm's _________ is then the composition or 'structure' of its liabilities. For example, a firm that sells $20 billion in equity and $80 billion in debt is said to be 20% equity-financed and 80% debt-financed.

a. Rights issue
b. Market for corporate control
c. Capital structure
d. Book building

13. In marketing, _________ is the process of distinguishing the differences of a product or offering from others, to make it more attractive to a particular target market. This involves differentiating it from competitors' products as well as one's own product offerings.

_________ is a source of competitive advantage. Although research in a niche market may result in changing your product in order to improve differentiation, the changes themselves are not differentiation.

a. 529 plan
b. 4-4-5 Calendar
c. 7-Eleven
d. Product differentiation

14. In finance, _________ (or gearing) is borrowing money to supplement existing funds for investment in such a way that the potential positive or negative outcome is magnified and/or enhanced. It generally refers to using borrowed funds, or debt, so as to attempt to increase the returns to equity. Deleveraging is the action of reducing borrowings.

a. Limited partnership
b. Pension fund
c. Financial endowment
d. Leverage

15. In business and accounting, _________s are everything of value that is owned by a person or company. The balance sheet of a firm records the monetary value of the _________s owned by the firm. The two major _________ classes are tangible _________s and intangible _________s.

a. EBITDA
b. Accounts payable
c. Income
d. Asset

16. In political economy and especially Marxian economics, _________ refers to one of four major attributes of a commodity, i.e., an item or service produced for, and sold on the market. The other three aspects are use value, value and price.

Thus, a commodity has:

- a value
- a use-value (or utility)
- an _________
- a price (it could be an actual selling price or an imputed ideal price)

These four concepts have a very long history in human thought, from Aristotle to David Ricardo, becoming ever more clearly distinguished as the development of commercial trade progressed. This entry focuses on Marx's summation of the results of economic thought about exchange-value.

a. Exchange value
b. A Random Walk Down Wall Street
c. ABN Amro
d. AAB

17. A _________ is a fungible, negotiable instrument representing financial value. They are broadly categorized into debt securities (such as banknotes, bonds and debentures), and equity securities; e.g., common stocks. The company or other entity issuing the _________ is called the issuer.

a. Securities lending
b. Security
c. Book entry
d. Tracking stock

18. A _________ is a discrete round of investment, by which a business or other enterprise raises money to fund operations, expansion, a capital project, an acquisition, or some other business purpose.

Hallmarks of an offering include the following (though none are an absolute requirement in every circumstance):

- A prospectus, private placement memorandum, or other document used to advertise the availability and terms of the offering, and to provide disclosure of information investors will need for their due diligence efforts
- A securities filing with relevant state and/or federal regulators
- Various contracts and documents by which the securities are sold such as a subscription agreement, a stock purchase agreement, and a convertible note (which documents a type of convertible security) or other loan document
- Various subsidiary or related agreements such as a buy-sell agreement, investor rights agreement, proxy agreements, and proposed amendments to a company's articles of incorporation
- Underwriters, brokers, finders, and/or agents who help sell and otherwise facilitate the investment transaction.
- Financial projections, financial statements, and projections and promises regarding the use of funds.

a. Common pool problem
b. Capital guarantee
c. Revaluation
d. Securities offering

19. A _________ is an event that may occur when a corporation's stockholders develop opposition to some aspect of the corporate governance, often focusing on directorial and management positions. Corporate activists may attempt to persuade shareholders to use their proxy votes (i.e. votes by one individual or institution as the authorized representative of another) to install new management for any of a variety of reasons.

In a _________, incumbent directors and management have the odds stacked in their favor over those trying to force the corporate change.

a. Forfaiting
b. Trade finance
c. Procurement
d. Proxy fight

20. A _________ is a statement required of a United States firm when soliciting shareholder votes. The firm needs to file a _________ with the U.S. Securities and Exchange Commission. This statement is useful in assessing how management is paid and potential conflict-of-interest issues with auditors.

a. 529 plan
b. 4-4-5 Calendar
c. 7-Eleven
d. Proxy statement

21. _________ is a corporate finance term denoting a type of takeover bid. The _________ is a public, open offer or invitation (usually announced in a newspaper advertisement) by a prospective acquirer to all stockholders of a publicly traded corporation (the target corporation) to tender their stock for sale at a specified price during a specified time, subject to the tendering of a minimum and maximum number of shares. In a _________, the bidder contacts shareholders directly; the directors of the company may or may not have endorsed the _________ proposal.

a. Tender offer
b. Follow-on offering
c. Cash is king
d. Shareholder value

22. In financial accounting, _________s are precautions for which the amount or probability of occurrence are not known. Typical examples are _________s for warranty costs and _________ for taxes the term reserve is used instead of term _________; such a use, however, is inconsistent with the terminology suggested by International Accounting Standards Board.

a. Momentum Accounting and Triple-Entry Bookkeeping
b. Money measurement concept
c. Petty cash
d. Provision

23. _________, also called fair price (in a commonplace conflation of the two distinct concepts), is a concept used in finance and economics, defined as a rational and unbiased estimate of the potential market price of a good, service, or asset, taking into account such objective factors as:

- acquisition/production/distribution costs, replacement costs, or costs of close substitutes
- actual utility at a given level of development of social productive capability
- supply vs. demand

and subjective factors such as

- risk characteristics
- cost of capital
- individually perceived utility

In accounting, _________ is used as an estimate of the market value of an asset (or liability) for which a market price cannot be determined (usually because there is no established market for the asset.) Under GAAP (FAS 157), _________ is the amount at which the asset could be bought or sold in a current transaction between willing parties, or transferred to an equivalent party, other than in a liquidation sale. This is used for assets whose carrying value is based on mark-to-market valuations; for assets carried at historical cost, the _________ of the asset is not used. One example of where _________ is an issue is a College kitchen with a cost of $2 million which was built 5 years ago.

a. 529 plan
b. 4-4-5 Calendar
c. 7-Eleven
d. Fair value

24. A _________ is an agreement between a company and an employee (usually upper executive) specifying that the employee will receive certain significant benefits if employment is terminated. Sometimes, certain conditions, typically a change in company ownership, must be met, but often the cause of termination is unspecified. These benefits may include severance pay, cash bonuses, stock options, or other benefits.
a. Trade finance
b. Debtor-in-possession financing
c. Market capitalization
d. Golden parachute

25. A mutual shareholder or _________ is an individual or company (including a corporation) that legally owns one or more shares of stock in a joint stock company. A company's shareholders collectively own that company. Thus, the typical goal of such companies is to enhance shareholder value.
a. Limit order
b. Stock market bubble
c. Stockholder
d. Trading curb

26. _________ is money paid by a company (or allied company or individual) to acquire its own shares of stock from a shareholder who is threatening to take control of, or unwanted influence of, the company.

The term is a neologism combining the terms greenback and blackmail, invented by journalists and commentators who saw the practices of corporate raiders as a form of blackmail. The target company is financially held hostage, and is legally forced to pay the _________er to go away.

a. Greenmail
b. 529 plan
c. Stock swap
d. 4-4-5 Calendar

27. In business and finance, a _________ (also referred to as equity _________) of stock means a _________ of ownership in a corporation (company.) In the plural, stocks is often used as a synonym for _________s especially in the United States, but it is less commonly used that way outside of North America.

In the United Kingdom, South Africa, and Australia, stock can also refer to completely different financial instruments such as government bonds or, less commonly, to all kinds of marketable securities.

a. Procter ' Gamble
b. Margin
c. Bucket shop
d. Share

28. In some countries, including the United States and the United Kingdom, corporations can buy back their own stock in a share repurchase, also known as a _________ or share buyback. There has been a meteoric rise in the use of share repurchases in the U.S. in the past twenty years, from $5b in 1980 to $349b in 2005. A share repurchase distributes cash to existing shareholders in exchange for a fraction of the firm's outstanding equity.

a. Common stock
b. Stockholder
c. Trading curb
d. Stock repurchase

29. A _________ is a payment made by a corporation to its shareholder members. When a corporation earns a profit or surplus, that money can be put to two uses: it can either be re-invested in the business (called retained earnings), or it can be paid to the shareholders as a _________. Many corporations retain a portion of their earnings and pay the remainder as a _________.

a. Dividend yield
b. Special dividend
c. Dividend puzzle
d. Dividend

30. In corporate finance, a _________ is a change of the capital structure of the company--usually to substitute debt for equity.

_________s are used by privately held companies as a means of refinancing, generally to provide returns to the shareholders while not requiring a total sale of the company. These types of recapitalizations can be minor adjustments to the capital structure or may involve a change of control.

a. Leveraged recapitalization
b. Bed Bath ' Beyond Inc.
c. Median
d. Modern portfolio theory

31. The _________ is a defensive option to stave off a hostile takeover in which a company that is threatened with a hostile takeover acquires its would-be buyer.

The most quoted example in U.S. corporate history is the attempted hostile takeover of Martin Marietta by Bendix Corporation in 1982. In response, Martin Marietta started buying Bendix stock with the aim of assuming control over the company.

a. Procurement
b. Golden parachute
c. Proxy fight
d. Pac-Man defense

32. _________, known in the United States as antitrust law, has three main elements:

- prohibiting agreements or practices that restrict free trading and competition between business entities. This includes in particular the repression of cartels.
- banning abusive behaviour by a firm dominating a market, or anti-competitive practices that tend to lead to such a dominant position. Practices controlled in this way may include predatory pricing, tying, price gouging, refusal to deal, and many others.
- supervising the mergers and acquisitions of large corporations, including some joint ventures. Transactions that are considered to threaten the competitive process can be prohibited altogether, or approved subject to 'remedies' such as an obligation to divest part of the merged business or to offer licences or access to facilities to enable other businesses to continue competing.

The substance and practice of _________ varies from jurisdiction to jurisdiction. Protecting the interests of consumers (consumer welfare) and ensuring that entrepreneurs have an opportunity to compete in the market economy are often treated as important objectives. _________ is closely connected with law on deregulation of access to markets, state aids and subsidies, the privatisation of state owned assets and the establishment of independent sector regulators. In recent decades, _________ has been viewed as a way to provide better public services.

a. Joint venture
b. Competition law
c. Securities Investor Protection Act
d. Fair Labor Standards Act

33. The Celler-Derek Browne Act is a United States federal law passed in 1950 that reformed and strengthened the Clayton Antitrust Act of 1914 which had amended the Sherman Antitrust Act of 1890. The _________ was passed to close a loophole regarding certain asset acquisitions and acquisitions involving firms that were not direct competitors. While the Clayton Act prohibited stock purchase mergers that resulted in reduced competition, shrewd businessmen were able to find ways around the Clayton Act by simply buying up a competitor's assets.
a. Celler-Kefauver Act
b. Fair debt collection
c. Private Securities Litigation Reform Act
d. Beneficial owner

34. The _________ of 1914, (October 15, 1914, ch. 323, 38 Stat. 730, codified at 15 U.S.C. Â§ 12-27, 29 U.S.C. Â§ 52-53), was enacted in the United States to add further substance to the U.S. antitrust law regime by seeking to prevent anticompetitive practices in their incipiency. That regime started with the Sherman Antitrust Act of 1890, the first Federal law outlawing practices considered harmful to consumers (monopolies and cartels).
a. National Securities Markets Improvement Act of 1996
b. Down payment
c. McFadden Act
d. Clayton Antitrust Act

35. The _________ of 1914 (15 U.S.C Â§Â§ 41-58, as amended) established the Federal Trade Commission (FTC), a bipartisan body of five members appointed by the President of the United States for seven year terms. This Commission was authorized to issue Cease and Desist orders to large corporations to curb unfair trade practices. This Act also gave more flexibility to the US congress for judicial matters.
a. Quiet period
b. Federal Trade Commission Act
c. Joint venture
d. Clayton Antitrust Act

36. The _________ of 1976 (Public Law 94-435, known commonly as the HSR Act) is a set of amendments to the antitrust laws of the United States, principally the Clayton Antitrust Act. The HSR Act was signed into law by President Gerald R. Ford on September 30, 1976. The context in which the HSR Act is usually cited is 15 U.S.C. Â§ 18a, title II of the original law.

a. 529 plan
b. Hart-Scott-Rodino Antitrust Improvements Act
c. 7-Eleven
d. 4-4-5 Calendar

37. The _________ was the first United States Federal statute to limit cartels and monopolies. It falls under antitrust law.

The Act provides: 'Every contract, combination in the form of trust or otherwise, or conspiracy, in restraint of trade or commerce among the several States, or with foreign nations, is declared to be illegal'. The Act also provides: 'Every person who shall monopolize, or attempt to monopolize, or combine or conspire with any other person or persons, to monopolize any part of the trade or commerce among the several States, or with foreign nations, shall be deemed guilty of a felony [. . .]'

a. 529 plan
b. 4-4-5 Calendar
c. Sherman Antitrust Act
d. 7-Eleven

38. Explicit _________ is a measure implemented in many countries to protect bank depositors, in full or in part, from losses caused by a bank's inability to pay its debts when due. _________ systems are one component of a financial system safety net that promotes financial stability.
a. Deposit Insurance
b. Reserve requirement
c. Banking panic
d. Time deposit

39. The _________ is a United States government corporation created by the Glass-Steagall Act of 1933. It provides deposit insurance, which guarantees the safety of checking and savings deposits in member banks, currently up to $250,000 per depositor per bank. Insured deposits are backed by the full faith and credit of the United States.
a. Ford Foundation
b. FASB
c. Federal Deposit Insurance Corporation
d. NYSE Group

40. The _________ of 1934 is a law governing the secondary trading of securities (stocks, bonds, and debentures) in the United States of America. The Act, 48 Stat. 881 (enacted June 6, 1934), codified at 15 U.S.C. Â§ 78a et seq., was a sweeping piece of legislation. The Act and related statutes form the basis of regulation of the financial markets and their participants in the United States.

a. 529 plan
b. 4-4-5 Calendar
c. 7-Eleven
d. Securities Exchange Act

41. The _________ refers to amendments to the Securities Exchange Act of 1934 enacted in 1968 regarding tender offers. The legislation was proposed by Senator Harrison A. Williams of New Jersey.

The _________ requires that bidders must include all details of their tender offer in their filing to the SEC and the target company. Their file must include the terms, cash source, and their plans for the company after takeover. There are also time constraints that stipulate the minimum period of time the offer may be open and the number of days after the offering in which shareholders have the right to change their minds.

a. Williams Act
b. Rule 144A
c. Securities Investor Protection Corporation
d. Prudent man rule

42. In finance, the _________ approach describes a method of valuing a project, company, or asset using the concepts of the time value of money. All future cash flows are estimated and discounted to give their present values. The discount rate used is generally the appropriate cost of capital and may incorporate judgments of the uncertainty (riskiness) of the future cash flows.
a. Net present value
b. Present value of benefits
c. Future-oriented
d. Discounted cash flow

43. In finance, _________ is the process of estimating the potential market value of a financial asset or liability. they can be done on assets (for example, investments in marketable securities such as stocks, options, business enterprises, or intangible assets such as patents and trademarks) or on liabilities (e.g., Bonds issued by a company.) _________s are required in many contexts including investment analysis, capital budgeting, merger and acquisition transactions, financial reporting, taxable events to determine the proper tax liability, and in litigation.
a. Share
b. Margin
c. Procter ' Gamble
d. Valuation

44. _________ is a measure of a company's earning power from ongoing operations, equal to earnings before the deduction of interest payments and income taxes.

To accountants, economic profit, or EP, is a single-period metric to determine the value created by a company in one period - usually a year. It is the net profit after tax less the equity charge, a risk-weighted cost of capital.

a. AAB
b. Economic profit
c. A Random Walk Down Wall Street
d. Operating profit

45. _________ is the difference between price and the costs of bringing to market whatever it is that is accounted as an enterprise (whether by harvest, extraction, manufacture, or purchase) in terms of the component costs of delivered goods and/or services and any operating or other expenses.

A key difficulty in measuring profit is in defining costs. Pure economic monetary profits can be zero or negative even in competitive equilibrium when accounted monetized costs exceed monetized price.

a. Economic profit
b. AAB
c. A Random Walk Down Wall Street
d. Accounting profit

46. The _________ is the rate that a company is expected to pay to finance its assets. WACC is the minimum return that a company must earn on existing asset base to satisfy its creditors, owners, and other providers of capital.

Companies raise money from a number of sources: common equity, preferred equity, straight debt, convertible debt, exchangeable debt, warrants, options, pension liabilities, executive stock options, governmental subsidies, and so on.

a. 4-4-5 Calendar
b. Capital intensity
c. Cost of capital
d. Weighted average cost of capital

47. In economics, business, and accounting, a _________ is the value of money that has been used up to produce something, and hence is not available for use anymore. In business, the _________ may be one of acquisition, in which case the amount of money expended to acquire it is counted as _________. In this case, money is the input that is gone in order to acquire the thing.

a. Cost
b. Marginal cost
c. Sliding scale fees
d. Fixed costs

48. The _________ is an expected return that the provider of capital plans to earn on their investment.

Capital (money) used for funding a business should earn returns for the capital providers who risk their capital. For an investment to be worthwhile, the expected return on capital must be greater than the _________.

a. Weighted average cost of capital
b. Cost of capital
c. Capital intensity
d. 4-4-5 Calendar

49. In finance, the _________ (continuing value or horizon value) of a security is the present value at a future point in time of all future cash flows when we expect stable growth rate forever. It is most often used in multi-stage discounted cash flow analysis, and allows for the limitation of cash flow projections to a several-year period. Forecasting results beyond such a period is impractical and exposes such projections to a variety of risks limiting their validity, primarily the great uncertainty involved in predicting industry and macroeconomic conditions beyond a few years.

a. Negative gearing
b. Terminal value
c. Refinancing risk
d. Discounted cash flow

50. _________s is a real estate appraisal term referring to properties with characteristics that are similar to a subject property whose value is being sought. This can be accomplished either by a real estate agent who attempts to establish the value of a potential client's home or property through market analysis or, by a licensed or certified appraiser or surveyor using more defined methods, when performing a real estate appraisal.

Five factors are usually considered when determining _________s:

- Conditions of Sale -- Did the _________ recently transact under conditions (e.g. -- arms length, distress sale, estate settlement) which are consistent with the standard of value under which the appraisal is being performed?
- Financing Conditions -- Was the _________ transaction influenced by non-market or other favorable (or even unfavorable) financing terms? For example, if the _________ sold with a below-market interest rate provided by the seller, and if the standard of value (e.g. -- market value) assumes no such abnormal financing, then the appraiser may need to adjust the _________ price by an amount equal to the estimated impact of the favorable financing.
- Market Conditions -- This is often referred to as the time adjustment and accounts for changing prices over time.
- Locational Comparability -- Are the _________ and the subject property influenced by the same locational characteristics? For example, even two houses in the same neighborhood may have different views which cause one to be more valuable than the other.
- Physical Comparability -- This includes such factors as size, condition, quality, and age.

A real estate appraisal is like any other statistical sampling process. The _________s are the samples drawn and measured, and the outcome is an estimate of value -- called an 'opinion of value' in the terminology of real estate appraisal.

a. Margin
b. Bucket shop
c. Comparable
d. Procter ' Gamble

51. _________ is a term used in modern English to indicate overweening pride, superciliousness often resulting in fatal retribution or nemesis. In ancient Greece, _________ referred to actions which, intentionally or not, shamed and humiliated the victim, and frequently the perpetrator as well. It was most evident in the public and private actions of the powerful and rich.
a. 7-Eleven
b. 529 plan
c. 4-4-5 Calendar
d. Hubris

52. A '_________' is a 'Charge' that is paid to obtain the right to delay a payment. Essentially, the payer purchases the right to make a given payment in the future instead of in the Present. The '_________', or 'Charge' that must be paid to delay the payment, is simply the difference between what the payment amount would be if it were paid in the present and what the payment amount would be paid if it were paid in the future.

a. Risk modeling
b. Value at risk
c. Risk aversion
d. Discount

53. The _________ is an interest rate a central bank charges depository institutions that borrow reserves from it.

The term _________ has two meanings:

- the same as interest rate; the term 'discount' does not refer to the meaning of the word, but to the purpose of using the quantity, such as computations of present value, e.g. net present value / discounted cash flow

- the annual effective _________, which is the annual interest divided by the capital including that interest; this rate is lower than the interest rate; it corresponds to using the value after a year as the nominal value, and seeing the initial value as the nominal value minus a discount; it is used for Treasury Bills and similar financial instruments

The annual effective _________ is the annual interest divided by the capital including that interest, which is the interest rate divided by 100% plus the interest rate. It is the annual discount factor to be applied to the future cash flow, to find the discount, subtracted from a future value to find the value one year earlier.

For example, suppose there is a government bond that sells for $95 and pays $100 in a year's time.

a. Stochastic volatility
b. Black-Scholes
c. Discount rate
d. Fisher equation

54. In finance and economics, _________ or divestiture is the reduction of some kind of asset for either financial goals or ethical objectives. A _________ is the opposite of an investment.

Often the term is used as a means to grow financially in which a company sells off a business unit in order to focus their resources on a market it judges to be more profitable, or promising.

a. Certificate in Investment Performance Measurement
b. Late trading
c. Portfolio investment
d. Divestment

55. _________ is the corporate management term for the act of reorganizing the legal, ownership, operational, or other structures of a company for the purpose of making it more profitable or better organized for its present needs. Alternate reasons for restructing include a change of ownership or ownership structure, demerger repositioning debt _________ and financial _________.

a. Restructuring
b. Day trading
c. Concentrated stock
d. Cross-border leasing

56. In law, _________ refers to the process by which a company (or part of a company) is brought to an end, and the assets and property of the company redistributed. _________ can also be referred to as winding-up or dissolution, although dissolution technically refers to the last stage of _________. The process of _________ also arises when customs, an authority or agency in a country responsible for collecting and safeguarding customs duties, determines the final computation or ascertainment of the duties or drawback accruing on an entry.

a. Liquidation
b. Debt settlement
c. 4-4-5 Calendar
d. 529 plan

57. A _________ is a new organization or entity formed by a split from a larger one, such as a television series based on a pre-existing one, or a new company formed from a university research group or business incubator. In literature, especially in milieu-based popular fictional book series like mysteries, westerns, fantasy, or science fiction, the term sub-series is generally used instead of _________, but with essentially the same meaning.

_________s as a descriptive term can also include a dissenting faction of a membership organization, a sect of a cult, or a denomination of a church.

a. 529 plan
b. 7-Eleven
c. 4-4-5 Calendar
d. Spin-off

Chapter 1

1. b	2. a	3. d	4. a	5. d	6. d	7. d	8. b	9. c	10. d
11. b	12. a	13. c	14. b	15. c	16. d	17. c	18. a	19. c	20. a
21. d	22. d	23. d	24. d	25. d	26. c	27. b	28. d	29. c	30. d
31. c	32. c	33. d	34. d						

Chapter 2

1. b	2. d	3. b	4. d	5. c	6. a	7. d	8. d	9. b	10. d
11. d	12. d	13. b	14. a	15. a	16. d	17. d	18. b	19. a	20. d
21. d	22. b	23. c	24. c	25. d	26. c	27. a	28. d	29. c	30. a
31. d	32. b	33. d	34. d	35. d	36. d	37. d	38. a	39. b	40. d
41. b	42. c	43. d	44. d	45. a	46. c	47. a	48. d	49. d	50. c

Chapter 3

1. d	2. d	3. d	4. c	5. d	6. b	7. c	8. d	9. d	10. c
11. d	12. a	13. d	14. d	15. d	16. b	17. c	18. d	19. b	20. a
21. a	22. b	23. d	24. a	25. c	26. d	27. b	28. d	29. b	30. d
31. d	32. c	33. d	34. d	35. b	36. c				

Chapter 4

1. d	2. c	3. d	4. b	5. b	6. c	7. d	8. a	9. a	10. c
11. d	12. a	13. d	14. b	15. a	16. c	17. d	18. b	19. d	20. a
21. d	22. d	23. d	24. d	25. d					

Chapter 5

1. d	2. d	3. d	4. d	5. a	6. d	7. d	8. d	9. d	10. d
11. d	12. d	13. d	14. a	15. d	16. c	17. d	18. d	19. b	20. d
21. c	22. d	23. b	24. b	25. d	26. a	27. a	28. b	29. c	30. b
31. d									

Chapter 6

1. a	2. b	3. d	4. d	5. d	6. a	7. d	8. c	9. d	10. d
11. a	12. a	13. a	14. d	15. c	16. b	17. b	18. d	19. b	20. b
21. d	22. a	23. d	24. d	25. b	26. a	27. b	28. b	29. c	30. d
31. a	32. d	33. d	34. d	35. b	36. c	37. a	38. d	39. b	40. b
41. d	42. c	43. c	44. d	45. d	46. c	47. d			

Chapter 7

1. a	2. b	3. d	4. d	5. d	6. d	7. d	8. d	9. a	10. d
11. b	12. a	13. a	14. d	15. b	16. b	17. d	18. a	19. d	20. c
21. d	22. b	23. b	24. d	25. d	26. a	27. a	28. a	29. d	30. b
31. d	32. b	33. d	34. d	35. a	36. a	37. a	38. d	39. b	40. d
41. b	42. d	43. c	44. a	45. d	46. d				

Chapter 8

1. d	2. b	3. d	4. d	5. d	6. d	7. d	8. b	9. a	10. d
11. a	12. c	13. d	14. d	15. d	16. a	17. b	18. d	19. d	20. d
21. a	22. d	23. d	24. d	25. c	26. a	27. d	28. d	29. d	30. a
31. d	32. b	33. a	34. d	35. b	36. b	37. c	38. a	39. c	40. d
41. a	42. d	43. d	44. d	45. d	46. d	47. a	48. b	49. b	50. c
51. d	52. d	53. c	54. d	55. a	56. a	57. d			

www.ingramcontent.com/pod-product-compliance
Lightning Source LLC
Chambersburg PA
CBHW081204240426
43669CB00039B/2807
* 9 7 8 1 4 2 8 8 7 2 0 0 4 *